NON-DECLARATIVE SENTENCES

Pragmatics & Beyond

An Interdisciplinary Series of Language Studies

IV:2

Richard Zuber

Non-declarative Sentences

NON-DECLARATIVE SENTENCES

Richard Zuber
Centre National de la Recherche Scientifique
(Paris)

JOHN BENJAMINS PUBLISHING COMPANY
AMSTERDAM/PHILADELPHIA

1983

For Kamil and Karol,
even though they might not read it

TABLE OF CONTENTS

ACKNOWLEDGEMENTS

I am indebted to many people for their help and advice. I forced Ross Charnock, Jeff Gould, and Ted Stazewski to correct the form of the book and my English. Often they also corrected the content. Oswald Ducrot made helpful and beneficial comments. These people are not responsible for most of the remaining errors. This book corrects and completes some of the ideas I have expressed elsewhere. As far as I can see, it is not in contradiction with what is presented in Zuber 1983a.

Given the form of the book, a complete reading is necessary for a full understanding.

0. INTRODUCTION

Undoubtedly, much progress has been made in the semantic analysis of declarative (sometimes also called indicative) sentences. The same cannot be said about non-declarative (non-indicative) sentences. At its beginning, the study of non-declaratives was misguided by the confusion, probably inherited from Austin, between the communicative values of illocutionary forces and speech acts as a part of social behavior on the one hand and the semantic values of linguistic expressions, outside of communicative and social interactions on the other hand. Due to this confusion, much has been learned about social and juridical changes caused by particular speech acts but rather little about the meaning of particular non-declarative sentences. Accidentally, the lexical content of various special lexical items – performative verbs – such as *to promise, to order, to ask,* or *to request* have become better known. But still, our knowledge of the semantics of non-declarative sentences has not increased.

In fact, the difficulty with non-declarative sentences is essentially due to the fact that they are formally (i.e. syntactically and morphologically) and especially conceptually much more complex than declarative sentences. This conceptual complexity of non-declaratives is deeply tied to their formal complexity, and more precisely to the fact that they are formally and, so to speak, qualitatively different.

Indeed, it is well-known that it is not at the lexical level that non-declaratives differ from declaratives; in most cases non-declaratives contain the same set of lexical items, and even of phrases, with the same grammatical functions as the corresponding declarative sentences. For instance, the exclamative sentence (1) and the interrogative sentence (2) have exactly the same set of lexical items fulfilling exactly the same grammatical functions in both sentences:

(1)   How fast Carol can run!
(2)   How fast can Carol run?

Similarly, the declarative sentence (3) and the interrogative sentence (4) do not differ in the lexical material they contain nor in the grammatical functions of their lexical items even though the two sentences clearly differ in meaning:

(3)   Carol can run fast.

(4)   Can Carol run fast?

Briefly, the difference in meaning between a declarative and a non-declarative sentence or between two non-declarative sentences of different types is not at all the same as the difference between the two following declarative sentences:

(5)   The dog sees the cat.

(6)   The cat sees the dog.

The semantic difference between (5) and (6) can be explained in terms of the difference in grammatical roles played by the corresponding lexical items in the two sentences, or in other words, by the fact that the two sentences do not have the same set of phrases, in particular verb phrases, with respect to the lexical material these VP's contain. Of course, the difference between declaratives and non-declaratives is not to be situated at this grammatical and lexical level. A semantic analysis of non-declaratives necessitates some new semantic rules: some higher order level of meaning, so to speak, must be involved in their analysis.

Various attempts to solve this difficulty have already been made. For a long time, logicians have been trying to reduce non-declarative sentences, at least interrogative ones, to declarative sentences. Their attempts were not taken too seriously, not even by themselves, I suspect.

Another more recent approach that is lexical in nature stems from Austin's work on performatives. Special lexical items, performative verbs, are used to 'give' the meaning of non-declarative sentences. For instance, the meaning of the interrogative sentence (4) may be 'given' by (7), a declarative in form:

(7)   I ask you whether Carol can run fast.

Clearly, (4) and (7) are semantically similar in many respects. But, clearly, they also differ, and not only in their form. Probably it is true of (4) that it 'asks' a question but it asks it in a different way than (7). It seems to me that an attempt must be made to explain this difference. Furthermore, to ask *why* (7) asks a question is probably as uninteresting as to ask why *artichoke* means 'artichoke' or why *artichoke* is translated into French as *artichaut*. On the other hand, the question *why* (4) 'asks' a question is not a trivial one and the answer to it may be very instructive. In my opinion, any theory of non-declarative sentences should try to answer this question in the same way as it should try to answer why (3), for instance, expresses an exclamation. It is not difficult to see that any purely performative approach to non-declarative sentences excludes such questions from its scope of investigation.

Another problem to which any theory of non-declarative sentences should address itself is that of the semantic relationship between a non-declarative sentence and the corresponding declarative one. There is a strong feeling that such relationships exist, and often, at least for some types of non-declaratives, this relationship is indirectly expressed. Thus, when one tries to determine what the notion of answerhood is, one clearly has to try to determine what the semantic relationship is between an interrogative and its corresponding declarative. Other non-declaratives also bear a systematic semantic relation to their declarative base. One is very much tempted to say that an exclamative sentence like (8) presupposes the corresponding declarative (9):

(8)   How beautiful Carol is!
(9)   Carol is beautiful.

Of course, for many people the notion of presupposition is far from acceptable, even for declarative sentences, so it might seem very courageous to speak of presuppositions of non-declaratives. I think, however, that non-declarative sentences also presuppose, and the fact that they presuppose the sentences that they do is very important for determining and understanding their meaning. In fact, the ancient thinkers of Megara were led to think about the presuppositions of questions a long time ago when they formulated one of their sophisms in the form of the question 'Have you lost your horns?'. As I will show, the presupposition of a non-declarative sentence is precisely the implication (or the semantic consequence) of all the 'indirect non-declarative' sentences derived from the given 'simple' non-declarative.

There is another problem with which any semantic theory of non-declaratives should deal. It concerns the number of possible types of non-declaratives. Given that the number of non-trivial boolean operations on a given declarative sentence (from which non-declaratives are constructed) is rather limited, the number of possible semantic relations which a non-declarative sentence can enter into with its declarative base is also very limited. So, if to every type of such a relation corresponds one type of non-declarative sentence, the number of different types of non-declarative sentences will also be very limited. And this is empirically correct: the number of different types of morphologically or syntactically marked non-declarative sentences is very limited, as compared to the number of performative verbs able to induce various illocutionary forces.

When we speak about indirect questions, orders, or exclamations, the following fact should be properly evaluated: all indirect non-declaratives are formed from an opaque (intensional) sentential operator in which a given non-declarative is embedded. These intensional operators are of the same type as the sentential operators containing propositional attitude verbs. For instance, verbs taking wh-complements or verbs taking interrogative or exclamative sentences as complements are verbs of propositional (more precisely cognitive) attitude. This fact, i.e. that no extensional sentential operators can apply to non-declarative sentences, is considered here as supporting the conclusion that neither non-declaratives nor the entities they express bear truth-values. This point of how the lack of truth-values is dealt with in natural language or how it is linguistically expressed cannot, I believe, be ignored in considerations concerning non-declaratives.

Of course, since intensional sentential operators can also take declarative sentences as complements, the study of indirect non-declaratives is connected in many respects with the study of some important phenomena from general semantics. In particular, a theory of non-declaratives must provide a way to account for the contribution subordinate non-declarative clauses make to the larger sentences of which they are parts. This requirement is precisely a natural consequence of the fact that non-declarative sentences can constitute clauses which can be syntactically embedded in larger sentences. This means that the study of non-declaratives must be a part of a more general field in which declarative and non-declarative sentences are uniformly treated; in particular, it must be a part of linguistic semantics.

In what follows, I will try to deal with the semantics of non-declaratives in the way indicated above, trying to construct the basis for a theory which may be able to answer the questions I consider any theory of non-declaratives should answer. In particular, I will try, in contradistinction to what has been done up to now, to analyze in a unified way all types of non-declaratives, interrogatives, imperatives, and exclamations, which, as I will show, in some sense exhaust the class of non-declaratives. To do this, I will first present various *intensional* semantic relations between two sentences. These relations are intensional in the sense that the first element of the relation, the implicating sentence, usually contains an intensional sentential operator in whose scope much lexical material occurs which is also found in the second element of the relation, the implied sentence. An example of such a relation is the relation between a factive construction and its sentential complement. A factive sentence is a complex sentence formed from an intensional sentential operator containing a propositional attitude verb which is applied to a declarative sentence constituting the complement of the factive sentence. Classically, the relation between a factive sentence and its complement is called *presupposition*. I will show that this denomination is justified. Furthermore, I will show that the presupposition relation is but a special case of intensional relations.

Since indirect non-declaratives are also constructed from intensional sentential operators applied to 'direct' or simplex non-declaratives, any semantic relation between an indirect non-declarative and a declarative containing some of the lexical material of the complement of the indirect non-declarative will be an intensional relation. Furthermore, it is possible to correlate various intensional relations with various intensional operators. The latter, in their turn, are correlated with different types of non-declaratives. So the study of intensional semantic relations has a direct application to the study of non-declaratives.

The results obtained in connection with intensional relations will also explain the differences in meaning between morphologically marked non-declaratives and the corresponding expressions containing explicit performatives.

Finally, in a less formal way and with some degree of speculation, I will try to show that there exists a presuppositional relation between a simple (indicative) conditional sentence and its antecedent.

There will be very little syntactic work in what follows. Somewhat arbitrarily, I will consider non-declaratives from the syntactic point of view as sentences. They can usually be distinguished from declarative sentences by formal — syntactical and/or morphological — markers, although I am aware that the exact choice of markers is rather arbitrary and that marking is neither necessary nor uniquely determines the type of non-declarative. The semantic description of non-declarative sentences which is proposed here is made on an abstract level although the exact status of this level is not specified. In any case, it is not the level of logical form, since, strictly speaking, no system of logic will be presented. I believe, however, that the description which will be proposed will serve as a basis of any precise and sound theory of non-declarative sentences and even of general semantics. In particular, the description proposed here will be necessary for understanding the entire complex phenomenon of non-declarative sentences.

1. INTENSIONAL RELATIONS

The intensional relations that I will present in this chapter are semantic implicative relations where the implying sentence is a complex sentence with an intensional operator which contains a lexical item in its scope that can also be found in the implied sentence. Schematically, an implicative intensional relation holds between a complex sentence O(P) and a sentence S — where O is an intensional sentential operator — when P and S have a lexical item of the nominal or sentential category in common and O(P) implies S. As generally accepted, we will say that a sentence S implies a sentence T iff in every situation in which S is true T is also true.

I will consider only operator expressions or function expressions, in the sense of categorial grammar, to be intensional or opaque. Furthermore, I will be interested primarily in unary (one place) operators. Consider now a complex expression formed from an operator expression applied to its argument expression . The intensionality (or opacity) of the operator making up the complex expression is manifested by the impossibility of replacing the argument expression of the complex expression by a semantically equivalent argument expression without inducing a change in the semantic value of the whole expression. The *semantic value* in this case is more strictly a 'logical value', *viz.* the extension. Since the argument expressions analyzed here will primarily comprise sentences and noun phrases, their semantic values will respectively be truth-values (denoted by sentences) and sets (denoted by noun phrases). Furthermore, semantic equivalence will be equated with extensional equivalence. Of course, when necessary, the methods of logical semantics can be used to generalize the extensions of other syntactic categories as functions of the extensions of their constituting categories.

With these specifications in mind we can introduce the following definition:

D1.0: Let O(A) be a complex expression formed from an operator expression O and an argument expression A. Then the operator O is opaque (or intensional) in the world (situation) w iff there exists another expression A´ of the same category and with the same extension as the category and extension of A such that $O(A)$ and $O(A')$ have different extensions.

Suppose one wants to apply this definition to operators O consisting of propositional attitude verbs as *Bill thinks that* or *Susan knows if*. These operators take sentences as arguments. Furthermore, they essentially involve human beings, that is, the grammatical subjects of the main VP's denote humans who are not omniscient but who nevertheless *know* something. It is then easy to find two sentences with the same truth-value (in the given world), P and P', such that $O(P)$ and $O(P')$ have different truth-values (in the given world). So, as expected, these operators are intensional. However, definition D1.0 poses a slight problem. Since it is not necessary that all humans exist in all possible worlds, the operator *Bill thinks that*, for example, ceases to be opaque in a world in which Bill does not exist; in such a world, (1) is false for every sentence P:

(1)   Bill thinks that P.

This is a rather undesirable consequence since we do not want linguistic properties like opacity to change with possible worlds. So definition D1.0 must be amended, so that it can at least account for the case of sentential operators and arguments.

Before proposing another definition of opacity for sentential operators, let me investigate a special case of implication between an intensional sentence (i.e. a complex sentence containing an intensional operator) and its complement sentence. Suppose that for any sentence P, the sentence $O(P)$ implies P. Then the law of contraposition does not hold for this implication: it is not true that *not-P* implies *not-O(P)*. Indeed, if O is opaque according to D1.0, there exists a sentence P' with the same truth-value as P such that $O(P)$ and $O(P')$ have different truth-values. Now, it can be easily verified that either *not-P* does not imply *not-O(P)* or *not-P'* does not imply *not-O(P')*. So, for an intensional implicative relation, the law of contraposition is not valid. It is well-known that the same is true of the presupposition relation with respect to the special type of negation used to define presupposition. We will see that this is the case for all intensional relations (with respect to the special 'normal' negation to be defined below).

The new definition of intensionality should take into account the fact that propositional attitude verbs normally have human subjects. This has two consequences. First of all, when the human being denoted by the subject of the verb does not exist, the complex sentence whose main verb has a human subject will always be false. Secondly, since human beings are not omniscient, one can always come up with a description or property of the object denoted by the noun phrase in the complement sentence of which the main subject is not aware. So one can always find an argument expression in the complement sentence which can be replaced by an equivalent one (with a different description) such that the replacement will make the whole sentence false.[1] Consequently, we have the following definition of *normal opacity*:

D1.1:   A sentential operator O is normally opaque iff
    (a) for some world w and some contingent sentence P, $O(P)$ is true in w;
    (b) for every possible world w and every sentence P, if $O(P)$ is true in w then there exists a sentence P' with the same truth-value as P in w such that $O(P')$ is false in w.

According to this definition, operators consisting of propositional attitude verbs and, consequently, operators taking non-declarative sentences as complements are normally opaque. On the other hand, the classical modal operators are not normally opaque. For instance, the operator *It is necessary that* is not normally opaque since there is no contingent sentence P and no world w such that *It is necessary that* P is true (in w).

Consider now the following sentences:

(2)   The bottle is half empty.

(3)   The bottle is half full.

These are logically equivalent sentences: they have the same truth-value in every possible world (given the present interpretation of English). However, embedding them in normally opaque operators can give different results depending on the operator: (2) and (3) can 'detect' the opacity of some operators but not of others:

(4) (a) Bill regrets that the bottle is half empty.
    (b) Bill regrets that the bottle is half full.

(5) (a) Bill knows that the bottle is half empty.
    (b) Bill knows that the bottle is half full.

It follows from these examples that the sentential operator *Bill regrets that* is 'more' opaque than the operator *Bill knows that* since its opacity is detected by sentence pair (2)-(3), whereas the operator *Bill knows that* is not 'sensitive' to this pair of equivalent sentences. So we can compare the relative degree of opacity of sentential operators. This can be done more precisely in the following way. Firstly, we say that the pair of equivalent sentences P and P' *detects* the opacity of the sentential operator O iff in some possible world w at which P

and P' have the same truth-value, $O(P)$ and $O(P')$ have opposite truth-values. Now we can introduce the following definition:

D1.2:   A sentential operator O is more opaque than a sentential operator O' iff every pair of sentences which detects the opacity of O' also detects the opacity of O, and there is a pair of equivalent sentences which detects the opacity of O but which does not detect the opacity of O'.

Notice that definition D1.2 permits us to compare normally opaque sentential operators with sentential operators which are not opaque (extensional). Clearly, any normally opaque operator is more opaque than an extensional operator, because no pair of sentences can detect the opacity of an extensional operator.

We can now easily define operators which are *equally* opaque: two operators are equally opaque iff any pair of sentences which detects the opacity of the first operator also detects the opacity of the second and, conversely, any pair which detects the opacity of the second operator also detects the opacity of the first. The sentential operators whose 'essential' lexical material is the same, e.g. *A knows that* and *A knows whether*, are equally opaque.

Note finally that two normally opaque sentential operators might not be comparable with respect to their degree of opacity: for every operator there may be a pair of sentences which detects the opacity of one operator but not of the other. Very likely, such incomparable operators can be constructed from the verbs *to know* and *to believe*.

My next step will be to introduce a concept of negation, which is essential in stating various properties of intensional relations. Syntactically, the negation we will use is the negation which applies to a sentential operator yielding a 'new' sentential operator. Semantically, such a negation may have various properties. In particular, it may preserve the opacity of the operator to which it is applied, or it may make it more opaque or less opaque than the operator to which it is applied. Whether all these possibilities are in fact realized in natural languages does not concern me here. I will be using primarily the opacity preserving negation. So we get the following definition:

D1.3:   An operational negation 'not' (i.e. the negation of the category (S/S)/(S/S)) is a normal negation iff
          (a) *not-O(P)* is true iff $O(P)$ is false;
          (b) *not-O* is a sentential operator equally opaque as the operator O.

In (6) we don't have a normal negation and, as will become more evident later, in (7) we do have a normal negation:

(6)   It is not true that Bill knows that *P*.

(7)   Bill does not know that *P*.

In natural languages, normal negations may be lexicalized. For instance *to ignore that* may be considered as the lexicalized normal negation of *to know that* and *to doubt that* as the lexicalized negation of *to believe that*.

By means of the notion of normal negation one can show that the following property holds (Zuber 1980c):

P1:   If *O(P)* implies *P*, for any sentence *P*, then *not-O(P)* implies *P*
       (where *O* is a normally opaque sentential operator and *not-O* its
       normal negation).

Suppose that property P1 does not hold. This would mean that there exists a world *w* in which *not-O(P)* is true and *P* is false. Since *not-O* is a normal negation, it would mean that there exists a sentence *P´* with the same truth-value as *P* such that *O(P´)* is true in *w*. But this is impossible because *O(P´)* implies *P´* and thus *P´* is true (in *w*). Consequently, property P1 is demonstrated.

Property P1 shows that normally opaque operators which have the property of implying their complement sentence behave like factive verbs: their negation also implies the complement sentence. Thus (8) and its normal negation (9) both imply (10):

(8)   Bill knows that Susan will call.

(9)   Bill does not know that Susan will call.

(10)   Susan will call.

It is possible to prove a more general property of which P1 is a particular case. Consider therefore that P1 relates not only an opaque sentence to its sentential complement but two complex sentences such that the first sentences contains an opaque operator which is more opaque than the operator in the second sentence. Indeed, the complement sentence *P* is equivalent to the complex sentence *It is true that P* and, as we noticed above, any opaque operator is more opaque than the extensional operator *It is true that*.

We now have two complex sentences of the form *O(P)* and *O´(P)*. Suppose that the opaque operators *O* and *O´* are comparable with respect to their degree of opacity. Then either *O* is more opaque, equally opaque, or less opaque than *O´*. For the first case, the following property P2 obtains (cf. Zuber 1982):

P2:   If *O(P)* implies *O´(P)*, for any sentence *P*, and *O* is more opaque
       than *O´*, then not-*O(P)* also implies *O´(P)*.

Suppose, *a contrario*, that P2 is false. Then there would exist a possible world *w* in which *not-O(P)* is true and *O′(P)* is false. Since *O* is more opaque than *O′*, *not-O* is also more opaque than *O′*. This means that there would exist a sentence *P′* with the same truth-value as *P* in *w* such that *not-O(P′)* and *O′(P′)* are false. But then *O(P′)* would be true which is impossible since *O(P′)* implies *O′(P′)*. It is clear that P1 is just a particular case of P2 where *O′* is the extensional operator *It is true that*.

As examples of complex sentences displaying property P2 consider (11), (12), and (13):

(11)   Bill regrets that Sue will call.

(12)   Bill does not regret that Sue will call.

(13)   Bill knows that Sue will call.

As we noticed above, *Bill regrets that* is more opaque than *Bill knows that*. Furthermore, (11) implies (13) and (12) is a normal negation of (11). So according to P2, (12) should imply (13). And this is empirically correct. To be precise, it means that sentences with emotive factive verbs as main verbs presuppose the corresponding sentence with the main verb *to know* (cf. Zuber 1977).

Let us now consider the case of opaque sentences with operators of the same degree of opacity. These sentences have the following property:

P3:   If *O(P)* implies *O′(P)* for any sentence *P*, and *O* and *O′* are equally opaque, then *not-O(P)* implies *not-O′(P)*.

This also will be proved *a contrario*. Suppose that there is a world *w* in which *not-O(P)* is true and *not-O′(P)* is false. This means that *O′(P)* is true in *w*. But then there would exist a sentence *P′* with the same truth-value as *P* in *w* such that *O(P′)* is true and *O′(P′)* is false. But this is impossible since *O(P′)* implies *O′(P′)*.

To illustrate property P3 consider (14) and (15):

(14)   Bill knows that Sue will call.

(15)   Bill knows whether Sue will call or not.

It is a fact that (14) implies (15). According to P3, (16) — the normal negation of (14) — should imply (17), the normal negation of (15):

(16)   Bill does not know that Sue will call.

(17)   Bill does not know whether Sue will call or not.

To be sure of this, notice that (15) is in fact equivalent to

(18)   Bill knows that Sue will call or Bill knows that Sue will not call.

Now, since *to know that* is a factive operator according to P1, (14) implies its complement sentence. This means that, when (16) is true, neither disjunct of (18) can be true, and consequently, (17) is true. Thus (16) implies (17).

The third possible implication between two opaque sentences remains to be examined, *viz.* when the second sentence has a more opaque operator than the operator of the first sentence which implies it. It can easily be shown that such a possibility cannot arise:

P4: It is not possible that a complex sentence $O(P)$ implies a sentence $O'(P)$, for any sentence P, where O' is more opaque than O.

Indeed, suppose that $O(P)$ implies $O'(P)$ and that O' is more opaque than O. Then there would exist a sentence P' logically equivalent to P in some possible world w such that $O(P')$ is true and $O'(P')$ is false. But this is impossible since $O(P')$ is supposed to imply $O'(P')$.

Up to now I have presented various possibilities which can arise between two opaque sentences of a particular form, namely when both sentences have the same complement sentence. It is possible, however, to consider a more general case, where both sentences have one argument expression in common, not necessarily the complement sentence. It may happen that a complex opaque sentence does not imply its complement sentence but a sentence which has only a nominal argument in common with the complement sentence. Take for instance (19) and (20):

(19) Bill thinks that the girl Sam met is my sister.

(20 Sam met a girl.

The common argument expression in the two sentences is the nominal *girl*. Two sentences related in this way can be called 'opaquely related sentences'. More precisely, the opaque sentence $O(P)$ is opaquely related to the sentence Q iff there exists an argument expression A in Q which is also in P. Then, depending on whether A is in the scope of an opaque operator in Q, and depending on the relative degree of opacity of this operator in comparison with the operator O in $O(P)$, we can show more general properties of which P1, P2, P3, and P4 are just special cases. In the proof one generally uses, instead of truth-values, the extensions of the nominal arguments A which the sentences have in common.

To see what the generalization of property P1 would look like, consider once again the last two sentences. There is a reading of (19) on which (19) implies (20). But on this reading, the normal negation of (19) also implies (20). In other words we get the following general property:

P1´:   If $O(P)$ implies Q, where $O(P)$ and Q are opaquely related sentences having a common argument A which is in the scope of O, and where O is more opaque than the operator having in its scope A in Q, then $not\text{-}O(P)$ also implies Q.

The proof is quite similar to that of P1.

Of course, it is not generally true that an implication relation holds between any two opaquely related sentences. In particular, as I will now show, an opaque sentence cannot imply the negation of its complement sentence (cf. Zuber 1982):

P5:   No opaque sentence of the form $O(P)$ can imply *It is not true that P.*

Following P2, because *It is not true that* is less opaque than O, $not\text{-}O(P)$ would also imply *It is not true that P.* Take a possible world w in which P is true. In this world $O(P)$ cannot be true. So in this world $not\text{-}O(P)$ is true. But this is impossible since $not\text{-}O(P)$ is supposed to imply the falsity of P.

The property just proved may be reformulated as asserting that there are no negative factives. In particular, contrary to what has sometimes been claimed, the (American English) verb *pretend (that)* is not a negative factive (although it is very likely to constitute a normally opaque operator in collocation with a grammatical subject). Property P5 will be used to analyze imperative sentences.

I have said above that intensional relations can be characterized as those implicative relations for which the law of contraposition is not valid. This is also true for the intensional relations described above, where the normal negation is taken into consideration. We have the following property:

P6:   If $O(P)$ implies $O´(P)$, for any sentence P, and $O´(P)$ does not imply $O(P)$, then it is not true that $not\text{-}O´(P)$ implies $not\text{-}O(P)$.

We know already that, if $O(P)$ implies $O´(P)$, then $O´$ cannot be more opaque than O (according to property P4). Consequently, either O is more opaque than $O´$ or O and $O´$ are equally opaque. Suppose that O is more opaque than $O´$. Then $not\text{-}O$ is more opaque than $not\text{-}O´$ (because the formal negation 'not' preserves the degree of opacity), and it is impossible for $not\text{-}O´(P)$ to imply $not\text{-}O(P)$ (following P4). Suppose now that O and $O´$ are equally opaque. Then, if $not\text{-}O´(P)$ implies $not\text{-}O(P)$, there exists a sentence $P´$ such that $O´(P´)$ implies $O(P´)$ which is excluded by the hypothesis.

In this first part, I have presented various particular cases of sentences entering into intensional implicative relations in order to approach the problem of presupposition from as general an angle as possible. The properties P1 and P2 show that it is possible to generalize the notion of presupposition by means of normally opaque operators. Consider once again the simplest case described by P1. Usually, factive constructions are said to presuppose their complement sentences. Indeed, we saw that if $O(P)$ implies P, then $not\text{-}O(P)$ also implies P – which is exactly what is meant by the notion of presupposition for factive constructions. Furthermore, we also know that the negation of P does not imply the normal negation of $O(P)$. But neither does $not\text{-}P$ imply $O(P)$ since O is more opaque than *It is not true that*. So what is happening here? The classical move is to say that $O(P)$ and $not\text{-}O(P)$ are neither true nor false when P is false. But another possibility is to say that when P is false, O or $not\text{-}O$ ceases to be normally opaque. And, in fact, it is a property of propositional attitude verbs that they can give rise to two readings (of the NP's in their scope). So, when a presupposition is false, a switch occurs from one reading to another or one reading is made impossible. Although, as I will try to make clear later on, the correspondence between transparent/opaque exists only for certain cases where arguments in the scope of opaque operators can have reference, it is possible to generalize the opaque/transparent distinction with the help of presupposition.

It follows from the properties presented above that a presupposition is just an intensional relation between two sentences such that the first sentence contains a normally opaque operator which is more opaque than the operator in the second sentence. But, as we know, the presupposition relation holds not only between opaque sentences; often sentences without any normally opaque operator can also have presuppositions, and clearly, in such cases, the above results are not directly applicable. Furthermore, we also want our definition of presupposition to apply to non-declarative sentences, interrogatives, imperatives, etc. The essential property of presuppositions of declarative sentences is that the presupposed content is independent of the truth-value of the presupposing sentence; there is a negation which does not operate on this type of semantic content. But non-declaratives do not have truth-values, and consequently, it is difficult to look for a semantic content which is independent of the the the 'truth-values' of non-declaratives. So one should look for an operator similar to the negation operator, but which can replace the negation, particularly in the case of non-declaratives. One property which such an operator should have is the property of not blocking presuppositions of simple sentences and allowing them to become presuppositions of complex sentences of which the simple sentences are parts. Another property is its metalinguistic character. It has often been noticed that the difference between presupposition 'creating' and presuppposition 'blocking' negations is metalinguistic in nature. A metalinguistic operator is also opaque and its opacity is of a very high degree. In any case, it is 'sensitive' to the linguistic form. But the phenomenon of opacity, or intensionality in general, is precisely expressed by the fact that opaque operators are form sensitive. In addition, normally opaque operators behave as presuppositional holes. Consider (21) and (22):

(21)   Bill regrets that John knows that Sue will call.
(22)   Sue will call.

It does not seem to be counterintuitive to consider (22) as a presupposition of (21). This means that the normally opaque sentential operator *Bill regrets that* allows the presupposition of the complement sentence of (21) to become the presupposition of the whole sentence (21). The same is also true of other non-factive, normally opaque operators. (23) also presupposes (22):

(23)   Bill believes that John knows that Sue will call.

Concerning the last example, one might object that (23) does not imply (22) because (23) may imply (24); in other words, (23) may have the meaning of (25):

(24)   Bill believes that Sue will call.
(25)   Bill believes that Sue will call and Bill believes that John knows that Sue will call.

Such a 'metalinguistic' reading of (23) is, however, excluded by the properties I have demonstrated. Indeed, since (23) and (24) are opaquely related, if (23) implies (24), then the normal negation of (23) should imply the normal negation of (24), but this would be empirically incorrect. In other words, normally opaque operators do not act as quotation marks or as metalinguistic operators. This seems to be true even for such operators as *to say that*. For instance, the meaning of (26) cannot be rendered by (27):

(26)   Bill said that the king of France is bald.
(27)   Bill said the following thing: "The king of France is bald."

So even (26) presupposes (on the most natural reading of *say*) what is presupposed by its own complement sentence. All this strongly suggests that in the new definition of presupposition the role played by the negation should be played by normal operators. And, indeed, this is the step I will take. The general definition of presupposition is the following:

D1.4:   A sentence P presupposes a sentence Q iff any sentence of the form
$O(P)$ implies Q, where O is a normally opaque sentential operator
for which there exists a normal negation.

The set of normal operators which is quantified over in the definition is closed
under the operation of normal negation.

Definition D1.4 has many advantages in comparison with the classical definition of presupposition. First of all, it applies to non-declarative sentences since
it is not necessary that the sentence P in the definition be a declarative sentence.
Secondly, it permits a more natural interpretation of sentences with false presuppositions, thus avoiding the use of a third truth-value: a sentence with a false
presupposition forces a non-opaque reading on a complex opaque sentence, i.e.
a reading in which an opaque operator whose complement is the sentence with a
false presupposition, loses its opacity. In other words, when a presupposition is
false, some complex opaque sentences do not have a normal negation. Finally,
this definition permits us to define other semantic relations which lie at the basis
of a better understanding of the 'meaning' of non-declaratives.

Before defining other relations applicable to non-declaratives, I would like to
show briefly by means of a few examples how the definition works for non-
declarative sentences. One may safely assume that the exclamative sentence (28)
presupposes (29) and that the interrogative sentence (30) presupposes (31):

(28)   How beautiful Sue is!
(29)   Sue is beautiful.
(30)   Who called?
(31)   Someone called.

Our definition of presupposition accounts for these cases. Indeed, all sentences
containing the exclamative sentence (28) as complement, such as (32), for
instance, imply (29), the presupposition in question. Similarly sentences in
which the interrogative sentence (30) is embedded, imply (31). As such, (33a)
and (33b) both imply (31):

(32)   Bill is surprised at how beautiful Sue is.

(33)(a) Bill is wondering who called.
     (b) Sue forgot who called.

Concerning declarative sentences, it can be shown that the above definition can
be simplified, given that the following is true: if a declarative sentence S presupposes a sentence T, then the sentence not-S also presupposes T (cf. Zuber n.d.).
This property thus corresponds to the definitional property used in the classical

definition of presupposition. It does not mean, however, that our definition permits us to obtain properties of presuppositions one gets from the classical definition. In particular, it is not true that presuppositions are transitive: it is not true that if P presupposes S and S presupposes T then P presupposes T.

Given definition D1.4 of presupposition, one can define other semantic relations between sentences. First of all, following Keenan (1973), we can define an assertion:

D1.5:   A sentence S asserts a sentence T iff S implies T and S does not presuppose T.

A declarative sentence asserts itself. Similarly, a conjunction of two sentences usually asserts each conjunct. Thus (34) asserts (35):

(34)   Bill arrived and Sue called.
(35)   Sue called.

In general, it is not true however that a declarative sentence asserts each of its non-presupposed implications. There is a class of declarative sentences which do not assert anything different from themselves; these are the so-called *analytic sentences*. An analytic sentence is a sentence which presupposes every consequence (implication) different from itself.[2] For instance (36) and (37) are analytic sentences:

(36)   The animal which was killed is dead.
(37)   Bill solved the problem he succeeded in solving.

Given our definition of presupposition, many 'positive', normally opaque operators are 'analytic' in that, when they are applied to an analytic sentence, they yield as a result another, more complex, analytic sentence. Thus (38) and (39) are also analytic sentences (cf. Zuber 1976) on their opaque readings:

(38)   Bill knows that the animal which was killed is dead.
(39)   Sue remembers that Bill solved the problem that he (=Bill) succeeded in solving.

The counterpart of an analytic sentence is a contradictory sentence: it is a sentence which presupposes the negation of all of its consequences which are different from the sentence itself. It can be shown that the normal negation of an analytic sentence is a contradictory sentence. Some 'inherently negative' normally opaque, sentential or non-sentential operators create contradictory sentences when applied to analytic sentences. This is probably the case with (40) and (41) on their opaque readings:

(40)   Bill doubts that the animal which was killed is dead.

(41)   Sue forgot to solve the problem which she succeeded in solving.

There exists a special class of assertions which may be called *proper assertions*. A sentence S properly asserts a sentence T (or T is a proper assertion of S) iff S asserts T and *not-S* asserts *not-T*. Normally, simple declarative sentences have only trivial proper assertions: they properly assert only themselves. We have seen, however, that opaque sentences can have proper assertions which are different from themselves; let us call such assertions *intensional proper assertions*. Indeed, we have seen (cf. P3) that, if $O(P)$ implies $O'(P)$ and O and O' have the same degree of opacity, then *not-O(P)* also implies *not-O'(P)*. This means for instance that (42) intensionally asserts (43) and (44) intensionally asserts (45):

(42)   Bill said that Sue called.

(43)   Bill said whether Sue called or not.

(44)   Bob forgot that the earth is round.

(45)   Bob forgot whether the earth is round or not.

Recall that, if S intensionally asserts T, it is not true that T asserts S, although *not-S* asserts *not-T*. This is so because the law of contraposition is not valid with respect to the normal negation which is used in the definition of intensional assertion. One can say, however, that S and T are intensionally equivalent since S implies T and *not-S* implies *not-T*. The idea of intensional equivalence will be made more precise below.

In fact, opaque sentences are not the only sentences to have intensional assertions. Thus, supposing that (46) presupposes (47), then (46) intensionally asserts (48):

(46)   Leslie is a poetess.

(47)   Leslie is a woman.

(48)   Leslie is a poet.

It is not true that all opaque sentences with *that*-complementizers have corresponding intensional assertions. The following two sentences very likely do not intensionally assert anything:

(49)   Bill regrets that Sue will not arrive.

(50)   Bob believes that the earth is round.

This is partially related to the fact that some verbs taking *that*-complementizers do not allow *whether*-complementizers. I will make use of this feature to characterize different types of non-declarative sentences, especially indirect non-declaratives.

With the help of the definitions of presupposition and assertion, it is possible to define some special equivalence relations. First of all, following Keenan (1973), we will define the relation of *being more explicit*:

D1.6:   A sentence T is more explicit than a sentence S iff S and T have the same set of consequences (implications) but some presuppositions of S are assertions of T.

Thus one can say that a more explicit sentence presents some of the presupposed content of the 'less explicit sentence' in the explicit and more 'accesible' form of an assertion. Consider the following illustrations:

(51)   Bill knows that Sue will call.
(52)   Sue will call and Bill knows whether Sue will call or not.
(53)   Sue will call.

Since (51) presupposes (53), (52) asserts (53), and moreover (51) and (52) mutually imply each other, according to definition D1.6, sentence (52) is more explicit than sentence (51). The so-called 'implicative verbs' provide another example. Compare the following sentences:

(54)(a) Bill tried to solve the problem and he solved it.
   (b) Bill succeeded in solving the problem.

Sentence (54a) is more explicit than (54b), since both are logically equivalent and (54b) presupposes the first conjunct of (54a).

There is an interesting analogy between explicit sentences and definitions (definitional sentences). A more explicit sentence is like a definition in that some of its terms are explicitly made more precise. This can be seen in examples (46)-(48), rephrased here in a more suitable form:

(55)(a) Leslie is a woman and Leslie is a poet.
   (b) Leslie is a poetess.

Sentence (55a) is more explicit than (55b) since it asserts the feminity of Leslie, the property which is left implicit in the form of a presupposition in (55b). At the same time, (55a) can be considered as a definition of *poetess* in (55b).

To illustrate the next relation between sentences, we will use examples similar to those above. This relation is the relation of *being privatively opposed*. We will adopt the following definition:

D1.7:   A sentence T is privatively opposed to a sentence S iff T is a proper intensional assertion of S (or S asserts intensionally T) and S has a presupposition absent from T.

The traditional view has it that only non-sentential categories can be privatively opposed. Thus a privative opposition involves a relation between two categories, or two terms, one marked and the other unmarked, for the unmarked category can be deprived of some semantic content which is present in the marked category. Thus Jakobson (1957: 9) presents this distinction informally as follows:

"The general meaning of marked category states the presence of a certain property A; the general meaning of the corresponding unmarked category states nothing about the presence of A and is used chiefly but not exclusively to indicate the absence of A."

In Zuber (1980a), I have tried to generalize the morphologically based distinction between a marked and an unmarked category to the sentence level by using in particular the notions of presupposition and assertion. In fact, according to definition D1.7, a privatively opposed sentence is nothing but an intensional assertion. It seems to me, however, that the intuition behind Jakobson's definition can also be accounted for in this way. Indeed, the property A referred to by Jakobson is a particular presupposition which is attached to the marked term and which is absent from the unmarked one. Thus *poetess* is the marked term in opposition to *poet* since it is possible to attach a particular presupposition 'woman' absent from the semantic content of the unmarked term *poet*. This move allows us to consider a privative opposition also at 'sentential level', since according to definition D1.7, sentence (56) is privatively opposed to sentence (57) and (58) is privatively opposed to (59):

(56)   Bill forgot whether Sue will call or not.
(57)   Bill forgot that Sue will call.
(58)   Bob knows whether it will rain or not.
(59)   Bob knows that it will rain.

Clearly, (59) implies (58) and (57) implies (56). The inverse implication does not hold: (56) does not imply (57) and (58) does not imply (59). Since, however, (56) and (57) both have a normally intensional operator with the same degree of opacity as do (58) and (59), according to property P3, the normal negation of (57) implies the normal negation of (56) and the normal negation of (59) implies the normal negation of (58). And this means that there is some kind of intensional equivalence between (58) and (59), for instance. And this equivalence expresses the very well known fact that an unmarked term can have the meaning of the corresponding marked one.

The equivalence in question is due to the fact that we are dealing with opacity preserving negation and not with 'extensional' or external negation. This negation, as we have seen, preserves presupposition. But what happens when presuppositions cannot be preserved and become false? Then a switch occurs in the meaning of the unmarked term: it acquires the 'meaning' which is in polar opposition to the marked term. In such cases, to use Jakobson's terminology, the unmarked category indicates the absence of the property whose presence is stated by the marked category. Thus the unmarked sentence (or sentence in privative opposition) is ambiguous, as its 'meaning' depends on whether the presupposition attached to the marked sentence (i.e. the sentence which intensionally asserts the unmarked sentence) is true or not. In a possible world in which such a presupposition is true, the unmarked sentence 'includes' the meaning of the marked sentence, and in a possible world in which the presupposition is false, the unmarked sentence (or rather one of its constituents) 'excludes' the meaning of the marked sentence (or rather of its corresponding marked constituent).

To illustrate this, we can take once again the classical example of *poetess* and *poet.* Consider the following set of sentences:

(60)   Leslie is a poetess.
(61)   Leslie is a poet.
(62)   Leslie is a woman.

When (62) is true, *poet* in (61) means 'poetess' or 'female poet'. In the worlds in which (62) is false, the unmarked noun *poet* cannot mean 'poetess' but only 'male poet'. A similar reasoning holds for sentences such as (58) and (59). In the world in which the complement sentence is true, *to know whether*, which can be considered as the unmarked constituent since it occurs in the privately opposed sentence, means 'to know that'. In other cases, *to know whether* means roughly 'to know that not'. And *to know that* is contrary to, and not contradictory to, *to know that not* in the same way as for instance the predicate *prince* is contrary and not contradictory to *princess.*

The idea of intensional equivalence between marked and unmarked sentences can be made more precise (cf. Zuber 1983b). In the marked and unmarked sentences, it is possible to replace a common argument (which is not in the scope of the opaque operator but which is semantically related to lexical material in the scope of it) by another one with the same extension so as to obtain two logically equivalent sentences. Thus in (60) and in (61) it is possible to replace Leslie by *this woman* or *John's sister* yielding (60´) and (61´), respectively:

(60′)   John's sister is a poetess.

(61′)   John's sister is a poet.

But the above two sentences are logically equivalent: they have the same truth-value in every possible world (given the present interpretation of English). A similar operation is possible with the opposition composed of the verbs *to know that* and *to know whether*. In (58) and (59), we can replace *Bob* by *the person who knows that it will rain* to get two logically equivalent sentences (58′) and (59′):

(58′)   The person who knows that it will rain knows whether it will rain or not.

(59′)   The person who knows that it will rain knows that it will rain.

Two other relations, more directly related to non-declarative sentences, remain to be explained. The first one concerns the possible reading of the sentence embedded in a normally opaque operator. It is well-known that various noun phrases in the scope of a propositional attitude verb can contribute to the reading of the whole construction in two ways: either the noun is taken directly, *de dicto*, or it is taken indirectly, *de re*, and it contributes to the interpretation of the whole construction implicitly, by the knowledge the speaker has in the form of presuppositions about the other NP's with the same semantic value. Thus, in (63), the noun phrase *Sue's sister* can be 'inserted' into the sentence by Bill himself, in his 'mental language', and then it is taken *de dicto* and its referent may not exist, or the NP can be put there by the speaker (and by the hearer, if necessary), and in the 'original' sentence *Bill* refers to the same already existing individual by another NP, in this case we have the *de re* reading:

(63)   Bill thinks that Sue's sister is leaving Paris.

Now, the complement sentence of (63) presupposes (64):

(64)   Sue has a sister.

This means that on the *de dicto* reading the opaque operator or its normal negation blocks the presupposition of the argument sentence. In this case, (63) is interpreted as (65):

(65)   Bill thinks that Sue has a sister and that Sue's sister is leaving Paris.

But such an interpretation of (63) is incompatible with the normal negation of (63). As one can easily verify, because of the presence of the conjunction in (65), the normal negation of (63) is not equivalent to the negation of (65). And this means that on the *de dicto* reading the definition of presupposition does not apply. Consequently, we get the following definition:

D1.8:   A complex opaque sentence *O(P)* has the *de dicto* reading given by the sentence *R* iff some presupposition of *P* is not implied by *R*.

We will see that this definition can also be applied to some readings of indirect non-declaratives.

Finally, I will define the notion of *declaration* – a relation between a sentence of whatever type and a declarative sentence. I propose the following definition:

D1.9:   A sentence *S*, of whatever illocutionary type, declares a declarative sentence *T* (or *T* is a declaration of *S*) iff
   (a) *T* is formally no more complex than *S*;
   (b) *S* and *T* have a common argument (nominal or sentential) able to detect the opacity of the operator in whose scope it may occur;
   (c) There exists a complex sentence containing *S* as its argument and asserting *T*.

So, roughly, a declaration corresponds to the semantic content which is not presupposed but which can be inherited by complex sentences containing the sentence the declaration of which we are analyzing. Furthermore, a declaration cannot be formally more complex than the declaring sentence. Indeed, there are many assertions of the given sentence which are inherited by complex sentences containing the given sentence, but which are more complex than the given sentence.[3] For instance, (66) and (67), a complex sentence containing (66) as argument, both imply and assert (68):

(66)   Sue will arrive.
(67)   It is true that Sue will arrive.
(68)   Sue will arrive or Bill will call.

According to the definition of declaration, however, (66) does not declare (68) because (68) is more complex than (66).

It follows from the example above that the declaration of any declarative sentence is at least its proper assertion, i.e., any declarative sentence declares itself. Declarative non-analytic sentences may have other declarations, formally simpler than themselves. Declarative analytic sentences declare only themselves. Furthermore, declarations, when restricted to declarative sentences, form a proper subset of assertions. Concerning non-declaratives, it will be shown later that they do not declare anything.

The concept of declaration can be used to generalize the relation of being *more explicit* so that this relation can be applied to non-declaratives as well. Indeed, it is clear that definition D1.6 cannot be applied to non-declaratives since it makes use of consequences or implications. The more general definition takes the following form:

D1.6´: A sentence T is more explicit than a sentence S, S and T being of whatever illocutionary type, iff
   (a) The union of the set of declarations and presuppositions is the same for S and T
   (b) There is a presupposition of S which is also a declaration of T.

I will use this definition in the next chapter when comparing explicit performative expressions with corresponding non-declarative sentences.

We are now sufficiently equipped to describe and to analyze non-declarative sentences. I have presented various semantic relations mostly between non-declarative sentences and declarative ones. The relations of presupposition and of declaration are the main relations that can hold between a non-declarative sentence and a declarative one; the relations of implication, of assertion, and of privative opposition hold only between declarative sentences. Since the most interesting properties of these relations concern complex opaque sentences, i.e. sentences containing a normally opaque operator, an analysis of opaque sentences seems to me particularly promising from this point of view. In particular, opaque sentences represented by indirect questions, indirect exclamations, and indirect orders will be analyzed in more detail in the following chapter by means of the privative opposition relation. It will be shown that the ambiguity between the 'illocutionary' or non-declarative and 'declarative' meaning of some indirect questions corresponds to the ambiguity between marked and unmarked readings and as such can be explained with the help of the privative opposition relation. In the last, more speculative, chapter I will try to show that in some metalinguistic sense, it is also possible to say that questions can be presupposed.

2. INDIRECT NON-DECLARATIVES

Since the semantics of non-declarative sentences apparently cannot be easily grasped, at least not by the usual methods, various indirect and reductionist methods have been proposed. The two best known approaches are those that make use of performative verbs or of verbs taking non-declarative sentences as complements. In the first part of this chapter, using some of the notions developed in the first chapter, I will criticize the performative approach, showing how it runs into various fundamental problems. In the second part, I will be concerned with the indirect non-declarative approach.

Although there is no question that the discovery of performative verbs and subsequent research on them contributed to a better understanding of human communication, it is far from evident that the study of language itself benefited from Austin's discovery to the degree speech acts theoreticians pretend it does. As Bierwisch (1980: 2) puts it, the original sin of speech act theory was to obscure the basic distinction between language and communication, two quite different aspects of human behavior. He convincingly shows that there are few reasons to consider speech act theory as an extension of a semantic theory of natural language: although partially interdependent, the two must not be confounded.

Developing some ideas put forward in Zuber (1981), I would like to show that the semantic identification of sentences which have a formal marking for mood with corresponding sentences that contain an overt performative verb results from the confusion between speech acts and the semantics of moods found in natural language, and consequently, this identification is not justifiable on semantic grounds.

We are accustomed, at least since Austin's work, to the fact that a given illocutionary force can be expressed in two linguistically different ways: by *mood markers* – syntactic and morphological devices used in natural language to construct interrogatives, imperatives, and other types of sentences, or by the use of performative verbs. The discovery of performative verbs and explicit performative expressions suggested some sort of equivalence between sentences with an overt mood marker and declarative sentences containing an explicit performative verb whose effect is to induce the illocutionary force of the corresponding mood. A number of logical and linguistic approaches to non-declarative sentences attempt to describe questions and orders, for example, by means of such performative verbs as *to ask* and *to order*. Apparently, a major argument for such claims is that the sentences in (1) are semantically identical:

(1) (a) I order you to close the door.
    (b) Close the door!

From a logical point of view, it is easy to find differences between the two types of sentences (cf. Gazdar 1976). Some of these differences can be described by means of relations introduced in the preceding chapter, in particular by means of the notions of presupposition and of assertion.

Before using the tools of presupposition and assertion, it is useful to point out that in some respects performative expressions differ notably from all non-performative expressions, whether declarative or non-declarative. The particularity of performative expressions I have in mind has to do with their token reflexive character or with the presence of various deictic elements. I will shortly point out two problematic aspects of their particularity.

It is a commonplace to consider the performative use of a verb, in opposition to its non-performative one, as essentially linked to the presence in performative expressions of the deictic first person I and the deictic present tense marker. Informally, the pronoun I is usually defined as designating the speaker or the person who says "I". The meaning of other deictic elements can be defined in a similar way. For instance, the deictic adverb *now* roughly indicates the moment at which the speaker says "now" (or utters the simple 'non-meta-linguistic' sentence containing the adverb *now*). An interesting question then arises: Does every grammatical category contain deictic elements? And more specifically: are there any deictic verbs? A deictic verb V, by analogy with deictic pronouns or deictic adverbs, is a verb V which expresses an action performed when the speaker says $I\ V(x)$, where x is the appropriate first person present tense marker. But clearly, this (very rough) description comes close to the description usually given for performative verbs. Indeed, consider (2), a prototypical performative expression:

(2)   I promise you to eat the artichoke.

The meaning of (2) is traditionally described in terms of the utterance of (2) itself and of the fact that the action expressed by the main verb is the action accomplished by uttering the verb *promise* (in 'deictic' terms, by the first person subject and in the present tense); promising is something one does by saying "I promise". Thus a performative verb is a deictic verb.

Now, it is possible to characterize deictic expressions by a special kind of presupposition. Consider

(3)   I am drunk.

If we think only about spoken language (and given the interpretation of the deictic I), it is normal to take (4) as a presupposition of (3):

(4)   Someone$_i$ said that he$_i$ is drunk.
        (There is an x such that x said that x is drunk.)

In other words, the deictic element I presupposes the existence of the sentence token in which I occurs. Consequently, since a performative expression such as (5) contains a deictic verb and the pronoun I, it can be characterized by the 'metalinguistic' presupposition (6), if we assume that, by definition, an action exists only if someone performs it:

(5)   I promise/advise/order you to call.
(6)   There is some x and some action A such that x said that x is doing (performs) A.

This presupposition characterizes performative expressions in general, irrespective of the performative verb used.[4] Non-performative expressions do not presuppose something like (6). This is obvious for expressions such as (7) and (8) that do not contain the deictic pronoun I:

(7)   He is writing a book.
(8)   He promises to call tomorrow.

It is also obvious for expressions which, although they contain the pronoun I, do not contain a performative verb:

(9)   I am writing a book.
(10)   I think that he must be stupid.
(11)   I am thinking that he must be stupid.

Here the existence of the person saying something is presupposed, but the existence of the action the speaker says he is doing is not brought about just by saying so, and furthermore, the speaker may be lying. Thus the presupposition of (5) says what a deictic main verb, or a sentence with the main verb in the first person singular present indicative 'means', while this verb supplies the name of the illocutionary act one would ordinarily be performing in uttering the sentence.

Since other sentences, whether declarative or not, do not contain deictic verbs, they do not have a particular presupposition expressing the specificity of the performative verb. This fact explains why Austin, and others after him, hesitated to call performatives statements or not. Austin held that they are not since they do not describe or report anything at all and, consequently, cannot be true or false. Austin's idea, although vague, was that performatives are in some way different from other verbs. This notion has been captured here by assigning a particular 'metalinguistic' presupposition to performative expressions, a presupposition due to the presence of a deictic verb.

Another aspect of the particularity of performative expressions has to do with so called 'sign transparency principle'. This principle, used sometimes in semiotics, states that signs do not draw attention to themselves but direct it to the extra-sign (extra-linguistic) reality. This principle is primarily connected with the so-called intentionality of psychic acts. The term *intentionality* was introduced in the philosophy of language and in semantics under the influence of Brentano's psychological theory. For Brentano, the main property of psychological acts is that they are always directed towards (non-linguistic) objects: one knows *something*, likes *something*, etc. . . This intentionality is thus a property of linguistic acts such that during speech production (or recognition) thought is directed to the objects referred to by the linguistic signs and not to the linguistic signs themselves. Husserl, and others, spoke about the transparency of any semiotic 'object' (sign), including sounds and graphic signs. Paintings in particular and pictures in general can also be considered as semantically transparent signs: what one perceives is not the physical or material aspect of the picture but the *world* symbolized by the author of the picture.

An interesting property of explicit performative expressions is that the principle of semantic transparency cannot apply to them: explicit performatives, treated as linguistic signs, are not semantically transparent (cf. Zuber 1979a). The basic argument which shows that explicit performatives do not conform to the sign transparency principle is based on the fact that deictic expressions cannot be semantically transparent and, as we have seen, performative verbs are deictic expressions. The meaning of a deictic expression directs the attention of the hearer to the expression itself as well as to the extra-linguistic reality. As we pointed out, in order to represent the meaning of deictic expressions, including performative verbs, it is essential to enclose the deictic in quotation marks: *I* is the person who says "I". But, clearly, quotation blocks transparency and directs the attention to the quoted segment. And, indeed, this is what happens when a performative sentence is used. Normally, when a non-performative expression is used, the attention of the participants in the conversation is directed not to the expression itself, but to the event, state, action, etc ... described by it. In the case of performative sentences, however, the state or action described by the sentence is created when the sentence is uttered. Otherwise the action in question does not exist. To utter a performative sentence is to create the action it 'describes'. It is not possible to attend to the action described without also attending to the sign which symbolizes it: the two are in some sense equivalent.

Let us consider the problem from another point of view. Given the presuppositions of deictic expressions described above, it is possible to paraphrase a performative sentence by a more explicit metalinguistic expression containing explicitly the verb *to say*. A such, (13a) and (13b) are more explicit than (12):

(12)   I promise to call.

(13)(a) I say "I promise to call."
    (b) I say that I promise to call.

The two more explicit sentences in (13) both contain opaque operators, which are thus sensitive to the linguistic form of their arguments. As a result, their interpretation is linked up with that form-sensitivity, thus invalidating the sign transparency principle when applied to performative sentences.

The above considerations of deixis and transparency in performative sentences help us to understand why the comparison of performative sentences with the corresponding non-declaratives have the same illocutionary force is in many respects nonsensical. Because of the presence of deictic elements, a semantic analysis of performative sentences necessarily involves the study of sign tokens, whereas the semantics of non-performative, in particular non-declarative sentences can be analyzed on the level of sign types. Of course, it is theoretically possible to circumvent the above differences by replacing deictic elements with non-deictic paraphrases. For instance, (14) can be replaced by (15) and then compared with (16):

(14)   I forbid you to close the door.
(15)   It is forbidden for you to close the door.
(16)   Don't close the door!

The problem, however, with this kind of reduction is that it does not always work, and when it does work it may lead to undesirable results. Transformations similar to the one above are not possible with many other performative verbs. For reasons which remain to be explained, forms like (17) and (18) are impossible:

(17)(a) *It is ordered that you close the door.
     (b)*One orders you to close the door.

(18)(a) *One asks whether you will phone.
     (b)*It is asked whether you will call.

Furthermore, in cases where the elimination of the deictic element is possible, important changes in meaning can result: (14) and (15) are far from having the same meaning.

Thus, from many points of view, performative sentences are incompatible with other types of sentences. But this does not mean performative and non-performative sentences are incompatible from all points of view. Very likely, performative sentences, in spite of the deictic elements they contain, can be treated as sentence types. In practice, speakers often put the two types of sentences on the same level. For this reason, it seems justified to me to describe the difference between performative sentences and morphologically marked non-declarative sentences in terms of the notions 'semantic presupposition' and 'assertion'. In this respect, I will make the following claim: the illocutionary force associated with a sentence whose mood is morphologically marked is *presupposed*, whereas the illocutionary force associated with an explicit performative sentence is stated explicitly or *asserted*. Thus I will say that in (19b) the order is presupposed, whereas in (19a) it is asserted. Similarly with (20): in the direct question (20b) the illocutionary force of interrogation is presupposed, whereas in (20a) it is asserted:

(19)(a) I order you to close the door.
     (b) Close the door!

(20)(a) I ask you (to tell me) who called?
     (b) Who called?

Of course, in order to be able to justify my claim, I need a general definition of presupposition, one that can apply to any sentence, whether declarative or non-declarative. The definition of presupposition I gave in the preceding chapter meets this required generality. It says, roughly, that one sentence presupposes another sentence iff every complex opaque sentence in which the first sentence is embedded entails (implies) the second sentence.

It is relatively easy to apply the above definition of presupposition to non-declarative sentences, because these sentences, whatever their type or illocutionary force, have declarative counterparts in the form of a complex sentence formed from the given non-declarative sentence plus a sentential operator which is normally opaque and which is applied to the given non-declarative sentence. To take a well-known example, all direct, morphologically or syntactically marked questions (interrogative sentences) have so-called indirect questions as their counterparts: (22b) and (21b) correspond to (22a) and (21a):

(21)(a) Who came?
    (b) We don't know who came.

(ss) (a) Will Bill come?
      (b) Susan doesn't remember whether Bill will come or not.

What is interesting is that, when taken together with their subject NP's, all question-embedding verbs, i.e. all and only those verbs which can be used to form indirect questions, form normally opaque sentential operators. Common among these verbs are *remember, forget, learn, notice, find out, guess, wonder,* etc ... It can easily be verified that all these verbs can give rise to normally opaque operators, partially because all of them involve knowledge in some sense, and moreover, because their human subjects are not omniscient, opacity naturally occurs. Thus for instance (23a) and (23b) can also differ in their truth-value even if *Susan* and *the girl I met* refer to the same person:

(23)(a) Bill learned whether Susan called.
    (b) Bill learned whether the girl I met called.

Since indirect questions can often be used with the same purpose as direct ones, or in other words, since indirect questions can carry the illocutionary force of interrogation in a way similar to that of direct questions, we can say, in an informal way, that indirect questions imply the illocutionary force proper to direct questions. That is, indirect questions imply the existence of their corresponding direct questions. But this means, according to our definition of presupposition, that this force is presupposed.

Imperative sentences can be analyzed in a similar way. Imperatives such as (24) correspond to opaque sentences such as (24a) or (24b):

(24)(a) Close the door!
    (b) I want you to close the door.
    (c) He wishes you to close the door.

Here again, the only verbs which can take 'direct' imperatives as complements are normally opaque verbs like *to wish, to want, to desire.* When such a direct imperative is embedded in one of these verbs, the illocutionary force of the order or command is preserved, which means that this force, according to our definition, is presupposed.

Finally, there is another class of non-declarative sentences which behave in a similar way. I am thinking of exclamations, as in (25) and (26), and optatives, as in (27):

(25)   How stupid he is!
(26)   How fast Bill can run!
(27)   If only she were pretty!

These non-declarative sentences differ from interrogatives and imperatives in that they do not have a performative counterpart. However, this does not prevent them — especially exclamations — from having indirect counterparts containing a normally opaque operator (cf. Elliott 1974; Grimshaw 1979). Thus the complements in (28) and (29) have an exclamative reading parrallel to the reading of respectively (25) and (26):

(28)   I am surprised at how stupid he is.
(29)   It is amazing how fast Bill can run.

Although exclamations can share their embedding verbs with questions in many cases, there exist various syntactic means for differentiating exclamations from questions in embedding constructions. However, for questions as well as for exclamations, the embedding verb with its subject can constitute a normally opaque operator. Since also in this case the complex sentences carry in general the illocutionary force of the formally (i.e. morphologically or syntactically) marked embedded sentences, it follows that this force is presupposed.

I would now like to give some additional, less formal arguments to support my claim. These concern the fact that presuppositions as well as illocutionary forces induced by formal marks can disappear in some contexts. Indeed, the illocutionary force of questions, for instance, is not always given directly by indirect questions:

(31)   I know who will come.
(32)   Steve discovered who did it.
(33)   She doesn't remember whether he won.
(34)   Steve asked whether John is stupid.

In indirect questions, the embedded interrogative sentences can lose the force of interrogation. Hence the questions in (31)-(34) do not require an answer in the way the corresponding embedded interrogatives do. In the same way, imperative sentences can lose the force of an order in some contexts:

(35)   Close the door if you want.
(36)   When he comes, close the door.

As I noted in the preceding chapter, normally opaque operators permit both an opaque and a transparent reading of their complement sentence. The most natural reading is the transparent one, but when the opaque reading occurs, as we have seen, the presuppositions of the complement sentence are blocked. For instance, (37) probably has the opaque reading given by (38), and on this reading (37) does not imply (39), which is a presupposition of the complement sentence:

(37)   Steve thinks that a girl who called didn't call.
(38)   Steve thinks that some girl didn't call.
(39)   A girl called.

Now, opaque readings, if possible, are possible when the main verb has a non-first person subject or is in a non-present tense; with the first person subject and present tense, the transparent reading is much more likely. But indirect questions do not normally express a request for an answer when they contain a non-first person subject.

There is another case where presuppositions can be canceled or neutralized. For example, such a presupposition neutralization can occur in certain contexts known as *filters* (Karttunen 1973; Zuber 1979b). Conditional sentences (or rather *if . . . then* connectives) are classical examples of filters. One can observe that in the context of an *if . . . then* connective, sentences whose mood is formally marked and their corrresponding sentences with explicit performative verbs do not behave in the same way. We have seen that this is true for imperative sentences, cf. (35) and (36). This is also true for interrogative sentences:

(40)   If I ask you who called, then who called?
(41)   If I promise you to come, who else will come?

Sentence (40) is very strange as to its pragmatic and semantic status; it does not seem to convey the force of a question and surely it does not request an answer; (41), on the other hand, is a question with a request for an answer. The difference between these two sentences can be easily understood if we recall the mechanism of presupposition neutralization by filters (i.e. by the *if . . . then* connective): the presupposition of the consequent clause is neutralized when it is semantically implied by the antecedent clause. According to the claim defended here, a morphologically marked question presupposes its interrogative force and the corresponding explicit performative sentence asserts its interrogative force. Consequently, the presupposed interrogative force of the consequent clause of (40) is neutralized, as the antecedent contains an explicit performative verb. In (41), the situation is different: the interrogative force of the consequent clause is not neutralized since the antecedent does not contain a performative verb with the same force as the consequent clause. Thus the illocutionary force presupposed by the consequent clause is not implied by the antecedent.

Another argument can be based on the behavior of adverbial clauses which can be used to detect presuppositions. It has been established that adverbial clauses usually modify the asserted and not the presupposed part of the 'argument' to which they apply. For instance, a *because*-clause usually modifies the assertion of the antecedent sentence:

(42)   Steve came alone because his wife is ill.

The *because*-clause in this sentence does not justify Steve's coming (presupposition) but his coming alone. This property of *because*-clauses can be used to support our claim:

(43)   Because I am your boss, I order you to close the door.

(44)   Because I am your boss, close the door.

(45)   Because you should be at home why are you here.

(46)   Because you should be at home, I ask you why are you here.

Sentences (44) and (45) are rather strange and require supplementary information for their interpretation, which is not necessary for the immediate interpretation of (43) and (46).

My next argument has to do with the negation of explicit performatives and the corresponding sentences morphologically marked for mood. The behavior of normal negation is, as we have seen, essential in detecting presuppositions: they are supposed to be outside the scope of normal negation, so to speak. When we compare the two types of constructions, *viz.* explicit performatives and mood markers, the desired differences appear. For instance, it is rather difficult to negate an interrogative or imperative sentence so as to deprive it of its illocutionary force. The following sentences must still be considered as interrogative or imperative:[5]

(47)   Who did not come?

(48)   Didn't he come?

(49)   Don't close the door!

Explicit performatives are known to lose their illocutionary force when negation is directly applied to them. Examples (50), (51), and (52) are clear in this respect:

(50)   I don't ask you to close the door.

(51)   I do not order you to close the door.

(52)   I do not promise you to come.

These sentences cannot be used to perform the speech acts corresponding to their performative verbs; illocutionary forces induced by overt performatives behave like assertions.

More generally speaking, one notices that embedding an explicitly performative expression in an opaque operator removes its corresponding illocutionary force. Thus (53), (54), (55), and (56) no longer carry the illocutionary forces one usually associates with their embedded sentences:

(53)   Bill regrets that I ask you whether she will call or not.

(54)   I think that I promise you to leave at midnight.

(55)   Bill knows that I order you to close the window.

(56)   He realizes that I advise you to write the letter.

This fact indicates that illocutionary forces carried by explicit performatives are not presupposed.

The last argument that I would like to mention concerns the possible existence of derived or indirect speech acts. We know that some sentences marked for one act can be interpreted as if they were marked for another, in principle different speech act. What is interesting is that this possibility only occurs with morphologically marked non-declarative sentences and not with sentences whose illocutionary force is induced by an overt performative verb. Thus only (57a) and not (57b) can be interpreted as an indirect order or request; (57b) remains a question in all situations:

(57)(a) Can you close the door?

     (b) I ask you (to tell me) if you can close the door.

Of course, it is still not entirely clear what is going on 'during' the derivation of indirect speech acts. Observe, however (cf. Zuber 1980b), that the derived speech act is usually based on the presupposition and not on the (intensional) assertion of the original, 'direct' speech act. For instance, (58) may indirectly express (59):

(58)   Do you have the New York Times.

(59)   Give/sell/lend me the New York Times.

On the other hand, (59) presupposes (60):

(60)   You have the New York Times.

Roughly speaking, *A gives/sells/lends B* presupposes *A has B*. This means that
the base (60) of (58), the sentence which gives rise to the indirect reading (59),
is in fact presupposed by (59). If this is indeed always the case (for more details,
see Zuber 1980b), then we can more easily understand the phenomenon
illustrated by (57a) and (57b): only the former sentence permits an indirect
interpretation, because this interpretation is based on its presupposed illocutionary force. The latter sentence asserts its illocutionary force and, therefore,
cannot serve as the basis for the derivation of an indirect act.

To conclude this section devoted to the presupposed character of illocutionary forces associated with non-declarative sentences, I would like to make
one clarification. What I have tried to justify is the claim that, unlike explicit
performative sentences, non-declarative sentences presuppose their illocutionary
force. This does not mean, however, that in some way the propositional content
of non-declarative sentences is also presupposed. The illocutionary force of
non-declarative sentences is presupposed *modulo* the truth-value of their
corresponding declarative base, so to speak. To see this point more clearly,
consider (61) and (62):

(61)   Close the book!
(62)   Don't close the book!

Both sentences presuppose the illocutionary force of a request or an order to do
something (with the book). It does not mean, however, that (61), for instance,
presupposes that there exists an illocutionary force requiring someone to close
the book since in that case (61) would, roughly speaking, presuppose itself.
Similarly, (62) does not presuppose the existence of the illocutionary force
requiring someone not to close the book. In other words, the 'illocutionary'
presupposition of both (61) and (62) is the same but there are evidently other
presuppositions which differentiate the two sentences. We will return to this in
more detail later.[6]

With respect to interrogative sentences, the situation is somewhat different
since, for at least some types of questions, some sort of equivalence exists
between the positive and negative forms of questions. Thus (63) and (64) are
in some sense equivalent:

(63)   Is it raining?
(64)   Is it not raining?

Because of this equivalence, it is possible to formulate a common 'illocutionary'
presupposition of both (63) and (64) in terms of something like (65):

(65)   There exists an illocutionary force of questioning whether it is raining or not.

In the following chapters, I hope to say more about these 'illocutionary' presuppositions.

A few things need to be said about the so-called 'indirect non-declaratives'. I will make only some general remarks here since various things have already been said and many others will be said in the following chapters.

Indirect non-declaratives are complex sentences formed from a normally opaque operator and a non-declarative sentence to which the operator applies. Clearly, it follows from this description that some explicit performative sentences are also indirect non-declaratives. This is so because performative verbs with a performative use constitute normally opaque operators. For instance, (66) is at the same time an explicit performative sentence as well as an indirect imperative sentence:

(66)   I order you to meet the president.

This example indicates that I am thinking about indirect non-declaratives in formal (syntactic) terms; semantically, (66) is a very 'direct' order.

Furthermore, if (66) is an indirect imperative sentence (in the above sense), then the non-sentential operator *I order you to* must be a (non-sentential) normally opaque operator. This indeed seems to be the case. A sentence similar to (66) in which an NP in the scope of the operator *I order you to* has been replaced by a co-extensional NP may have a different truth-value; (67) and (66) may differ in their truth-value even if *the president* and *my neighbor* refer to the same person:

(67)   I order you to meet my neighbor.

More generally, performative verbs seem to constitute opaque operators only when they are used performatively, i.e. when they are used with the first person and in the present tense. The two following sentences always have the same truth-value when their noun phrases refer to the same person:

(68)   He ordered you to meet the president.
(69)   He ordered you to meet my neighbor.

This fact is probably connected with the existence of the particular 'deictic' presupposition which one should associate with performative verbs.[7]

As opposed to performative sentences, opaque sentences, i.e. sentences containing a normally opaque operator, need not have a first person subject or be in the present tense. Moreover, they can even have an 'indirect human subject', as in (70) or (71):

(70)   It seems that Bill has left

(71)   It is well-known that linguistics does not exist.

The indefinite subject *it* in these constructions indirectly evokes humans since *to seem* or *to be well-known* must involve judgments and consequently human beings.

So, clearly, the class of opaque operators is much larger than the class of performative expressions. This becomes even more obvious if we realize that many opaque operators have no corresponding performatives. In particular, there is no corresponding performative for exclamative sentences. Indeed, neither (72) and (73), nor any other sentence containing a sentential complement and directly or indirectly expressing an exclamation based on its complement sentence can be considered as an explicit performative:

(72)   I am surprised at how stupid he can be.

(73)   I am amazed what a beauty she is.

But, clearly, these sentences are indirect exclamatives. This fact suggests that studying non-declaratives *via* indirect non-declaratives is more appropriate than studying them through performatives.

Now I would like to say a few words about the role of different complementizers found in different types of indirect non-declaratives. Up to now, we have primarily been occupied with sentential operators applying to non-declaratives. It is well-known, however, that operators do not occur indiscriminately in collocation with all complement types; they cannot take all types of non-declaratives as arguments. Moreover, as Grimshaw (1979) convincingly shows, in order to account for complex constructions with sentential complements, subcategorization restrictions, which are syntactic in nature, must be completed with semantic selection restrictions between operators and the semantic or illocutionary type of their complements. Operators do not select complements of a particular syntactic form but rather complements of a particular semantic type. This means that indirect non-declaratives are categorized not only according to the type of their complement sentence but also according to the form of the complementizer which introduces the given complement.

Some opaque operators display an interesting 'ambiguity': they can take two different complementizers which, roughly, introduce either declarative complements or only one type of non-declarative complements: we have *to know whether* vs. *to know that* or *to find out whether* vs. *find out that.* Thus we can say that (74) are indirect questions whereas (75) are 'indirect declarative sentences':

(74)(a) Bill will find out whether it rains often.
    (b) Sue knows whether the earth is flat.

(75)(a) Bill will find out that it rains often.
    (b) Sue knows that the earth is flat.

These two sets of sentences only differ in the complementizer used. On the other hand, operators corresponding to other kinds of non-declaratives do not display this type of ambiguity. Thus operators applying to exclamative sentences or to imperative sentences cannot take two different complementizers. For instance, only (76a) is possible:

(76)(a) I am surprised that he is so stupid.
    (b)*I am surprised whether he is so stupid.

So we are now obliged to investigate whether this formal difference between indirect interrogatives on the one hand and indirect imperatives and indirect exclamations on the other hand yields a semantic difference between the two classes of indirect non-declaratives.

It is possible to investigate the semantic impact of the above difference by means of the notion of privative opposition I have defined in the preceding chapter. I have suggested that constructions with a *whether*-complementizer should be considered as being privatively opposed to their corresponding constructions with a *that*-complementizer. Given this fact, we can formulate the above difference between indirect non-declaratives in the following way: only indirect questions enter into privative oppositions; indirect imperatives and indirect exclamations lack the corresponding unmarked constructions. Furthermore, indirect questions entering into privative opposition should be considered as the unmarked term of the opposition. Consequently, only indirect questions can display the ambiguity inherent to the unmarked term in a privative opposition.

Let me recall what the ambiguity is I have in mind. Remember that (77) is the unmarked member in its opposition to (78):

(77)   Leslie is a poet.
(78)   Leslie is a poetess.

Sentence (77) has an unmarked 'literal' meaning which asserts that someone named Leslie, either a man or a woman, is writing poetry. In this case, abstraction is made from the sex of the person, and consequently, on this reading it is not presupposed that Leslie is a man or that Leslie is a woman. But in a special situation, maybe with a special intonation, (77) can be used to carry the information that Leslie is a man — in such a case, we are dealing with the polar opposition to the marked sentence (78); on this reading, the presupposition of (77) is precisely the negation of the 'marking' presupposition of (78).

The ambiguity of the unmarked construction becomes probably more clear when we consider its negation: (79), the negation of (77), can mean either (80), the normal unmarked or 'literal' meaning, or (81), the 'derived' meaning:

(79)   Leslie is not a poet.

(80)   Leslie is a woman but not a poet.

(81)   Leslie is not a poetess but a poet.
        (i.e., Leslie is not a woman.)

Here also the 'non-literal' reading is based on the presupposition of the marked construction (77).

A similar, but more complex reasoning holds for indirect questions; more complex because indirect questions may be privatively opposed to two 'marked' constructions. Schematically, as we have seen, *O whether P* may be privately opposed to *O that P* and to *O that not-P*. Thus sentence (82) can be the unmarked counterpart of (83) as well as of (84):

(82)   Bill knows whether the earth is flat.

(83)   Bill knows that the earth is flat.

(84)   Bill knows that the earth is not flat.

The normal unmarked reading of (82) is the reading which asserts that Bill has some particular knowledge about the earth. On this reading, neither the complement of (83) nor the complement of (84) are implied. On the other hand, (82) can have an 'indirect' or marked reading on which a request for an answer is made. This request is induced by the fact that on this reading the truth of one of the complements, either the complement of (83) or that of (84), is presupposed. These complements express the presuppositions of the marked constructions. Thus the request for an answer corresponds to the request for establishing which complement or which presupposition, positive or negative, is presupposed by the unmarked sentence.

What I have just said implies that indirect non-declaratives which do not enter into privative oppositions should not have the two readings indirect questions have. This means that indirect imperatives and indirect exclamations, since they do not enter into privative oppositions, are not ambiguous in the way indirect questions are. And, indeed, this seems to be the case. For instance, (85) can hardly have a 'literal' meaning; it always carries the force of an order:

(85)   Bill wants you to leave early.

Similarily with indirect exclamations: (86) cannot be just a statement; it always expresses an exclamation:

(86)   Bill is surprised at what a large library I have.

Furthermore, even some indirect questions have only one reading, in which, roughly, the request for an answer is expressed. It happens when there is no corresponding marked form with a *that*-complementizer, or when that form is semantically ill-formed. For instance, since (87) is impossible, (88) does not carry the meaning of a simple statement:

(87)   *Bill wonders that the medecine can help him.
(88)   Bill wonders whether the medecine can help him.

Similarly, the prevailing interpretation of (89) and (90) is that of a question and not of a simple informative statement.

(89)   I don't know whether he will call me or not.
(90)   Bill wants to know whether logic is amazing.

This is because the corresponding marked constructions (91) and (92) are in principle ill-formed:

(91)   I don't know that he will call me.
(92)   Bill wants to know that logic is amazing.

Thus the class of indirect non-declaratives contains syntactically and semantically different members. The difference between them can be analyzed by means of some intensional relations that were introduced in the first chapter. We will see that the different behavior of various types of indirect non-declaratives leads to similar differences at the level of *direct* non-declaratives. In particular, we will see that only rhetoric questions exist and that there are neither rhetoric imperatives nor rhetoric exclamations.

3. UNDERSTANDING QUESTIONS

Among non-declarative sentences, interrogatives are the type that have most frequently aroused a deep interest among researchers studying various phenomena of natural language. I will, therefore, begin the study of proper or direct non-declaratives with interrogatives. To do this, I will chiefly use the generalized notion of presupposition which was introduced in the first chapter and some results about indirect non-declaratives obtained in the preceding chapter. I will also review, briefly but critically, various other approaches to the study of interrogatives,

First, let me recall a simple terminological convention that is sometimes used and that concerns the difference between questions and interrogative sentences. A question is the semantic content of an interrogative sentence. By analogy with declarative sentences and propositions, a question is similar to a proposition, which is the semantic content of a declarative sentence. Questions, like propositions, are supposed to be language-independent, whereas interrogatives and declaratives exhibit a particular linguistic form determined by the grammar of the given language. Evidently, all these notions can only be given a precise meaning within a general theory, but this is beyond the scope of my considerations.

I should add that I may not always respect the terminological distinction above. However, this should not give rise to any particular confusion.

Probably everybody interested in language was once puzzled by the status of questions as linguistic entities. There are many reasons why questions can be fascinating and surprising. For logically oriented semanticists the main reason for this fascination seems to be as follows: among the various predicates which apply to declarative sentences (in linguistic terminology) or to statements (in logical terminilogy), two in particular cannot apply to questions. A question cannot be true or false. In other words, questions are one of the first representatives that come to mind when one speaks about non-declarative sentences.

In fact, we know of various linguistic entities to which the predicates *true* or *false* are not applicable. For instance nouns, or names, or more generally, noun phrases (in linguistic terminology) are such objects. Furthermore, often some sentences of natural language play the role of sentential functions containing a 'free variable' (a pronoun) and as such they are neither true nor false. Moreover, in some other cases, certain declarative sentences do not have truth-values or do not make any statement — these are sentences with false presuppositions. But normally, nobody would say that questions are entities that belong to one of these types — there seems to be no obvious reason for considering questions as nouns (verbs, adjectives, etc.), as simple sentential functions, or as declarative sentences with false presuppositions. They must be taken as different objects, in some way deprived of their truth-values.

The fact that questions cannot be associated in a straightforward way with truth-values is not without importance for those interested in the logical form of linguistic expressions. This fact, when recognized, obliges logicians to look for various alternatives that reduce questions in some way to objects which can be dealt with in propositional logic or class calculus.

Thus the first generation of erotetic logicians — logicians of questions — tried to replace questions in an unique way by declarative sentences or classes or such sentences, and then to operate on those (declarative) sentences in the well-known way.[8] For these logicians the essence of a question is in some way given by the set of its (possible, direct, true, proper, etc.) answers. For instance, Hamblin (1958) states that "Knowing what counts as an answer is equivalent to knowing the question."

Let me make a few comments about this approach to the study of questions. It somehow assumes that questions cannot be studied in isolation, separated from their answers. This is far from evident. To take an analogy from the study of pronouns or sentential functions, one agrees that pronouns can be usefully studied, up to some point, without studying their antecedents. The same may be true of questions: it is a priori possible that they can be studied without reference to their answers.

Furthermore, from an intuitive point of view, many answers are better when they are given not in the form of a whole sentence but in the form of an appropriate part of the sentence. For instance, (2) is more appropriate as an answer to (1) than (3) because (3) is in some way redundant and often odd:

(1)   Who came yesterday evening to see Sue?
(2)   Henry.
(3)   Henry came yesterday evening to see Sue.

Another important fact in this respect is what counts as an answer to a given question. For instance, (5) is a more appropriate answer to (4) than (6) or (7) even if (as we suppose) (6) and (7) express the same proposition as (5):

(4)   Did Henry eat the artichoke?
(5)   Yes, Henry ate the artichoke.
(6)   Yes, the artichoke was eaten by Henry.
(7)   Yes, the artichoke was eaten by the guy who came yesterday.

Furthermore, no propositional erotetic logic takes into account the fact that any answer to a *yes-no* question must contain the particle *yes* or *no* at the beginning. This fact seems really important for conditions on answerhood, and in connection with other mentioned facts, it clearly indicates that answers are not just propositions or statements. Thus, even if Hamblin's dictum, which was given without any justification, is true, questions cannot be understood if they are simply considered as classes of declarative sentences or statements that are studied with the classical means.

Another approach, more interesting for us from the cognitive point of view, is the one put forward by Aqvist (1965) and then developed by Hintikka (1974, 1978) and to a certain extent by some linguists (Wachowicz 1978; Lang 1978). According to this approach, a question is a kind of epistemic request. For instance, the question (8) can be paraphrased by something like (9a) or (9b):

(8)   Will Henry come?

(9) (a) Let it be known whether Henry will come or not.
    (b) Bring it about that I know whether Henry will come or not.

In fact to be more precise, the Aqvist-Hintikka approach to the logic of questions uses the very well developed apparatus of the logic of imperatives and of epistemic logic, and both logics provide an interesting and powerful framework in which the paraphrases of type (9) can be precisely expressed. So, from the formal point of view, there cannot be any objection against this type of paraphases of questions. It can be criticized, however, with respect to its psychological aspects. First of all, it is far from evident that the epistemic element used in the paraphrases is in any way characteristic of questions. It is indeed possible that the epistemic element is due to the presence of the disjunction *or* somewhere in the logical form of the question. It has often been noticed that when uttering a sentence containing a disjunction a speaker wants to imply that he is not in a position to precisely specify the alternatives offered by the sentence with the disjunction. For instance, (10) informally implies (11):

(10)   Tegucigulpa is the capital of Honduras or of Costa Rica.
(11)   The speaker does not know exactly of what country is Tegucigulpa the capital.

Thus the element of knowledge (or rather of ignorance) used in the Aqvist-Hintikka paraphrase of questions may not belong to the primitive or literal 'meaning' of questions but probably to its derived, secondary meaning. The same may be true of the imperative element used in the paraphrases (9).

Furthermore, one can observe (cf. Zuber 1978c) that the use of the imperative operator *let* does not necessarily make the paraphrase more comprehensible than the question itself. Indeed, grasping the 'meaning' of an order may appear as difficult as grasping the meaning of a question. Thus, psychologically speaking, the paraphrases in (9) are not necessarily more explanatory than (8) itself. On the other hand, from a technical point of view, (9a) is intensionally more explicit than (8): some presuppositions of (8) might appear to be intensional assertions of (9a).

Notice in addition that this last point of criticism applies to the idea put forward by some linguists who want to explain the meaning of a question, or at least who want to derive a question from its corresponding performative expression (as for instance Harris (1978)). Some details of this problem are given in the preceding chapter.

From looking at these introductory remarks, it should have become clear what the purpose of this chapter is. I would like to propose an analysis of questions which avoids, at least in my mind, the objections I have just made in connection with some of the previous approaches to interrogative sentences and questions. In particular, an interrogative sentence and the question it expresses will be considered in isolation from the answer, of any kind whatsoever, to the question. Furthermore, the approach I will put forward is semantic rather than pragmatic in nature. In other words, I will not employ the notion of the speaker or of the person who 'asks' the question, or of the person who answers the question, or more generally, of the person who performs a particular speech act.

It will become clear that my ideas of the 'logic of questions' are not novel at least in one respect: they are uncontroversial in regarding a question as involving a disjunction of mutually exclusive disjuncts — a question, formally considered, certainly *is* a disjunction. The novelty of my proposal, as far as I can see it, consists in changing the nature of the disjuncts. Indeed, I will consider a question not as a disjunction of assertions, or directly of statements, but as a disjunction of presuppositions. And this fact makes a question different from an 'ordinary' disjunction of statements and, as we will see, permits us to retain the distinctive feature of questions, namely their interrogative character.

Questions can be considered in this way by 'extracting' simple direct questions from indirect questions, which are not primarily questions but statements.

In fact, even if it is not so evident that indirect questions are not questions (in their 'literal' meaning), I will only use the observation that direct questions are embedded in sentences that are indirect questions. It is precisely this syntactic fact and not its semantic consequences, that I will need.

The extraction of a question from its corresponding indirect question is made possible through the generalized notion of presupposition presented in the first chapter. In addition, I will need for this purpose the two following properties of presuppositions: any semantic consequence of a presupposition of a given sentence is also a presupposition of this sentence and, secondly, if a sentence S presupposes another sentence then the negation of S also presupposes the same sentence.

Before specifying conditions on which an expression can be said to express a question, I will state an important restriction on possible truth-values of some complex sentences. This restriction concerns the truth-values of the complement sentences of factive constructions: two factive constructions which have the same opaque operators but mutually contradictory complements cannot be true in two different possible worlds. More precisely, there are no two possible worlds w_i and w_j such that $O(P)$ is true in w_i and $O(not\text{-}P)$ is true in w_j. Thus (12) and (13) cannot be true at the same time in two different possible worlds:

(12)   Bill knows that P.
(13)   Bill knows that $not\text{-}P$.

In other words, factive presuppositions have, in some sense, rigid denotations. The analogy with the notion of rigid denotation of proper names is fundamental to the above restriction. It is possible, however, to give a linguistic justification for this restriction along the following lines. Factive constructions such as (12) or (13) are possible marked counterparts of their corresponding constructions with a *whether*-complementizer or of their corresponding indirect questions. This means that indirect questions enter into privative opposition with factive constructions. Now, a privative opposition is a linguistic or semantic property of some expressions belonging to a language with a fixed interpretation and, as such, it cannot change with possible worlds. It is clear that in a given possible world only one marked counterpart, either $O(P)$ or $O(not\text{-}P)$, can be true. Consequently, if we agree that the marked counterpart in a privative opposition relation cannot change with possible worlds, we are obliged to accept the above restriction.

We are now in a position to establish the necessary and sufficient conditions for an expression to express a question. For the time being, I will restrict myself in this analysis to what is usually called a *yes-no* question since I consider it in some sense a basic question that is essential for the understanding of all other kinds of questions.

I will begin by establishing a useful terminological convention I will need in describing *yes-no* questions: any *yes-no* question is *based* on or has as a *base* a sentence which is, roughly speaking, the corresponding declarative sentence. Schematically, the question *Q(S)* is *based* on or has as a *base* the sentence *S*. For instance, the base of the question (14) is sentence (15):

(14)   Will Henry come?
(15)   Henry will come.

As I already indicated, I will avoid establishing any direct correspondence between the base of a *yes-no* question and its (possible, direct, true, etc.) answers.

What is a necessary condition for a *yes-no* question? Suppose we have the question (14) and we derive from it a 'simple' indirect question (16):

(16)   Bill knows whether Henry will come.

I will not discuss the possible syntactic problems that may arise from considering (16) as an indirect question in which (14) is embedded. Suffice it to say that this is in agreement with traditional and not so traditional analyses of indirect questions.

What now are the semantic consequences or entailments of (16)? Intuitively, *to know whether S* means 'to know that *S* or to know that *not-S*'. More precisely, one obtains the same result if one decomposes the *know whether* sentences into *know that* sentences according to the following pattern: (17) is equivalent to (18) which has (19) as a semantic consequence:

(17)   A knows whether *S*.
(18)   If *S*, A knows that *S* and if *not-S*, A knows that *not-S*.
(19)   A knows that *S* or A knows that *not-S*.

Sentence (19) follows from (18) on the assumption that *know that S* sentences entail the corresponding embedded sentences *S*: *A know that S* entails *S*. By the same entailment one obtains (20) as the next step:

(20)   *A knows whether S* entails *S* or *A knows whether S* entails *not-S*.

Notice that the 'double' entailment indicated in (20) is not a trivial one: it is not true that entailed sentences are tautologies (*S or not-S*). Moreover, it is not generally true that a declarative sentence either entails another sentence *S* or that it entails the negation *not-S*.

Now, according to property P1 (cf. chapter 1), the normal negation of (17) also entails *S* or *not-S*. In other words, (21) is also true:

(21)   *A does not know whether S* entails *S* or *A does not know whether S* entails *not-S*.

My next step is to show that the entailment similar to the one given in (20) holds not only for sentences with *know-whether* but also for any other indirect interrogative sentence. In other words, we have to show that something like (22) is also true:

(22)   *O whether S* entails *S* or *O whether S* entails *not-S*.
        (where *O* is a question embedding operator)

Karttunen (1977) gives a list of question embedding verbs used in forming question embedding operators. When one looks at the various verbs this list contains, one notices that every verb on the list, if it can be used to form an indirect question, either entails *to know whether* or entails *not to know whether*. For instance, the sentences in (23) entail (24) and those in (25) entail (26):

(23)   A found out/informed/remembered whether *S*.
(24)   A knew whether *S*.
(25)   A learned/wondered/asked whether *S*.
(26)   A did not know whether *S*.

It should be clear now how (22) can be justified. Since every question taking operator either entails *to know whether* or *not to know whether*, and since (21) is true, by the transitivity of entailment, (22) must also be true.

I have just shown that every indirect interrogative sentence (in the positive or in the negative form; cf. property P1) either entails the base of the embedded question or it entails the negation of the base of the embedded question. But since the only opaque operators which can be applied to interrogative sentences are operators containing question embedding verbs, this means that all opaque sentences in which a question with a given base *S* is embedded entail either the base *S* or the negation of the base *S*. But this last statement, in conjunction with the definition of presupposition, precisely entails that a *yes-no* question with base *S* either presupposes *S* or presupposes *not-S*. Consequently, we get the following necessary condition for a question:

(27)   The *yes-no* question *Q(S)* either presupposes *S* or presupposes *not-S*.

We can show that (27) is also a sufficient condition. Before doing this, let me introduce the following definition:

D3.1:   A sentence S maximally presupposes a sentence P iff every presupposition of S is entailed by P.

Notice that the presupposition corresponding to the base of the *yes-no* question described in condition (27) is a maximal one. To show that (27) expresses also a sufficient condition, suppose that the condition stated by (27) and completed by D3.1 holds for an expression E. In other words we have (28):

(28) E maximally presupposes sentence S or E maximally presupposes *not-S*.

Some expressions trivially presuppose S or *not-S* because they presuppose just S, e.g. factive constructions with complements S. These factive constructions do not maximally presuppose S, however, since one can associate with them some other, existential presuppositions. We already know that the unmarked counterparts of factive constructions, i.e. sentences with a *whether*-complementizer, imply, and even presuppose, either their (declarative) complement sentence or the negation of that complement. Also in this case, supplementary, existential presuppositions are carried by indirect interrogatives. As in the case of factive constructions, these existential presuppositions are due to the existence of the human referent of the subject NP's of the question taking verbs. For instance, (29) presupposes not only its declarative complement (the base of the embedded question) but also the additional information given in (30):

(29)   Bill knows whether it will rain.
(30)   There is someone named Bill.

Because of the additional presuppositions, neither factive sentences nor their unmarked counterparts, i.e. indirect interrogatives, can be considered by condition (27) as direct interrogatives. And this is empirically correct: factives and indirect interrogatives are formally in no way interrogative sentences.

What does it mean to say that an expression E satisfies condition (28)? According to the definition of presupposition, this means that every opaque sentence $O(E)$ containing E as its complement either maximally implies a declarative sentence S or it maximally implies *not-S*. If we consider any opaque sentence of the form $O(E)$, the additional presupposition of type (30) should be common to all opaque sentences but this is impossible since, when opaque operators vary, the subject NP's of the corresponding verbs also vary. Consequently, by varying the opaque operators in the way required by the definition of presupposition we avoid the unnecessary additional presuppositions that are not related to the complement sentence.

I have just established that all opaque operators which can take E as complement are necessarily *whether*-complementizer taking operators. But this means that E is an interrogative sentence since only these operators take questions as complements. Consequently, if an expression E satisfies condition (28), E is an interrogative sentence with base S.

We can express the essence of the above results by the following definition:

D3.2:   An expression E is a *yes-no* question with base S iff E presupposes S or E presupposes *not-S*.

I will make some comments about definition D3.2 at the end of this chapter when presenting general ideas about the notion of questions here proposed. For the moment, I would like to approach some other types of questions in a similar way.

The procedure that I used for *yes-no* questions can be easily extended to the so-called *alternative questions*. An example of such a question is given in (31):

(31)   Will Bill come or will Sue call?

This question has two bases, *viz.* (32a) and (32b):

(32)(a) Bill will come.
   (b) Sue will call.

To simplify things, I will say that the base of the alternative question (31) is a two-member base. Theoretically, the base of an alternative question can have any finite set of members: $S_1, \ldots, S_n$. An alternative question based on such an n-member base will be noted as $Q(S_1, \ldots, S_n)$.

There are of course also indirect alternative questions. An example of an indirect alternative question corresponding to the direct alternative question (31) is given in (33); in (34) we find an example of an indirect alternative question with the n-member base indicated above:

(33)   Joe asks whether Bill will come or Sue will call.
(34)   A knows whether S_1 or $\ldots$ or S_n.

We already know that, according to property P1, any indirect interrogative sentence of type (34) can imply, and even presuppose, one of the disjuncts of its complement sentence. This leads us to the following definition of an alternative question:

D3.3: An expression E is an alternative question with base $S_1 \ldots S_i$ $\ldots S_n$ iff either E presupposes $S_1 \ldots$ or E presupposes S_i or $\ldots$ or E presupposes S_n

Notice that by analogy with *yes-no* questions, the disjunction in D3.3 is an exclusive disjunction: only one disjunct of the form 'E presupposes S_i' is true. Furthermore, an alternative question should not be confused with a multiple question. A multiple question is a conjunction of 'simple' *yes-no* questions. For example, (35) is a multiple question different from the alternative question (31):

(35)   Will Bill come and will Sue call?

Although probably semantically related to it, this question is still different from the *yes-no* question (36) whose base is a conjunction of the two bases of (35):

(36)   Will Bill come and will Sue call?

The two definitions of questions, D3.2 and D3.3, enable us to rediscover some well-known properties of 'simple' questions. The first property concerns the presuppositions of a *yes-no* question and its base: these presuppositions are identical. Indeed, suppose that the base S of a question $Q(S)$ presupposes a sentence P. Then the question $Q(S)$ presupposes either S or it presupposes *not-S*. If $Q(S)$ presupposes S then it also presupposes P since S presupposes P. And if $Q(S)$ presupposes *not-S* then it also presupposes P, because *not-S* presupposes P.

The second property which we can obtain from definition D3.2 concerns the possible equivalence between 'positive' and 'negative' *yes-no* questions. It is usually assumed that on its 'literal' reading, (37) is equivalent to (38):

(37)   Didn't he call?
(38)   Did he call?

More generally, there is an equivalence between a question $Q(S)$ and a question $Q(not-S)$. This equivalence can be obtained in the following way. The question $Q(S)$ is fully described by (39) and the question $Q(not-S)$ is fully described by (40):

(39) $Q(S)$ presupposes S or $Q(S)$ presupposes *not-S*.

(40) $Q(not-S)$ presupposes *not-S* or $Q(not-S)$ presupposes *not-(not-S)*.

Since the presupposition we are talking about in (39) and in (40) is a maximal one and since *not-(not-S)* is equivalent to S, one can consider the descriptions in (39) and (40) as describing equivalent questions.

Various semantic relations we have studied in connection with declarative sentences could be used to define similar relations for questions. For instance, one could define *a void question* as a *yes-no* question whose base is an analytic sentence; (41) would be an example:

(41)   Has the girl who has called called?

An impossible question would be a question with a contradictory base, as in (42):

(42)   Has the girl who has called not called?

Various particular properties of *void* or *impossible* questions could be studied making use of semantic relations. It seems to me, however, that this would not really be a study of interrogative sentences or of questions but rather a study of declarative sentences. So I will not pursue this direction. I will only mention one possible application of the semantic relations we have discussed to the study of some properties of questions. In my opinion, using the notion of *the more explicit sentence*, it is possible to approach the problem of the relative difficulty of *yes-no* questions.

When speaking about the difficulty of questions, we should keep in mind the fact that not all questions can be comparable from the point of view of their difficulty. Clearly, it would be somewhat unnatural to try to compare the relative difficulty of (43) with that of (44):

(43)   Was it raining yesterday?
(44)   Is Bill a good linguist?

These two questions have logically independent bases. Now, if we want to compare questions we should be able to compare the bases of the questions: the events or states of affairs described by the bases should be the same. For instance, the two following questions are comparable since their bases are logically connected:

(45)   Did Bill sell a car to Jim?
(46)   Did Jim buy a car from Bill?

These two questions are not only comparable with respect to their relative difficulty, but they are probably equally difficult: to answer the first question, one needs as much 'research' and deduction as to answer the second one.

There are, however, declarative sentences which, although logically equivalent, do not yield questions with the same difficulty. Consider (47) and (48):

(47)   Sue called and Bill knows whether Sue called or not.
(48)   Bill knows that Sue called.

It seems to me that the question based on (47) is more 'difficult' than the question based on (48); thus (49) is more 'difficult' than (50):

(49)   Is it true that Sue called and Bill knows whether Sue called or not?

(50)   Is it true that Bill knows that Sue called?

Roughly speaking, one can say that (49) is more 'difficult' than (50) because the base of (49) is a conjunction; and, in fact, (49) is composed in some sense of two questions, each based on one of the two conjuncts of the whole base (47). In other words, we should answer (49) twice whereas one simple answer to (50) is sufficient.

We already know that sentence (47) is related to (48) by the relation of 'being more explicit': (47) is more explicit than (48) because (47) and (48) are logically equivalent and (47) asserts a sentence that is presupposed by (48). The same sentence is presupposed by (50) and 'questioned' by (49), and consequently, (49) has more 'semantic material' to question than (50).

The above remarks lead to the following definition:

D3.4:   A question $Q(S)$ is more difficult than a question $Q(T)$ iff the base S is more explicit than the base T.

The above definition tries to connect some semantic properties with other properties which are psychological in nature. As such, it may be useful for a better understanding of what entity a question represents.

Up to now, we have essentially been occupied with questions having a sentential or propositional base. In some sense, these questions correspond to the level of propositional calculus. We know that there are also questions explicitly implying a quantification and as such they correspond to predicate calculus. These are the so-called wh-questions illustrated by the following set of examples:

(51)   Who called yesterday evening?

(52)   Which linguist does not work on universals of language?

(53)   When will Bill arrive?

(54)   Why is life so sad?

(55)   Whom did you meet?

A wh-question is characterized by the presence of an interrogative pronoun or a question phrase specifying a certain syntactic category. The question phrase takes the position the corresponding category takes in the related declarative sentence and is often moved to front-position. The category of the question phrase is the same as the category of possible answers to the wh-question.

It seems very natural from a syntactic point of view to treat interrogative pronouns and determiners such as *who* or *which* in the same way as 'declarative' pronouns (determiners) such as *every, some, the,* etc. Indeed, they often assume the same position in the phrase or they display a similar agreement in gender, number, etc. What is more important, however, is the fact that *wh*-determiners and *wh*-pronouns show the semantic properties characteristic of declarative determiners and, in particular, that they behave like quantifiers. The similarity of *wh*-determiners and pronouns to declarative determiners was shown in detail in Keenan and Hull (1973). In particular, they noticed that both types of determiners bind pro-forms in the same way, as the following set of examples shows:

(56)(a) Some linguist loves himself.

    (b) Every linguist loves himself.

    (c) Which linguist loves himself?

Furthermore, *wh*-questions and quantified sentences show similar scope ambiguities. Thus conjoining two *wh*-phrases differs semantically from *wh*-questioning a conjunction in the same way as conjoining two quantified phrases differs from quantifying into a conjunction. This is illustrated by (57) and (58) respectively:

(57)(a) Which linguist wrote the paper and which linguist stole the book?

    (b) Which linguist wrote the paper and stole the book?

(58)(a) Some linguist wrote the paper and some linguist stole the book.

    (b) Some linguist wrote the paper and stole the book.

Given this analogy between interrogative and declarative quantifiers, we can describe the former by the methods we use to describe the latter. At least since Peirce, it has been admitted that usual declarative quantifiers are just abbreviations of conjunctions or disjunctions of a particular form. Thus (59) is an abbreviation of (60):

(59)   All A's are B.

(60) a_1 is B and a_2 is B and ... and a_n is B.

The existential quantifier *some* on the other hand is an abbreviation of an (inclusive) disjunction. As such, (61) abbreviates (62):

(61)   Some A's are B.

(62) a_1 is B or a_2 is B or ... or a_n is B.

Exactly what does 'abbreviation' mean in these cases? In (59) or (61), the sets that are quantified over are not specified although they are in some way implicitly known and given. On the other hand, in the case of the explicit conjunction and disjunction, the elements of the quantified set are explicitly specified: they are $a_1 \ldots a_n$. We can say that in the latter case the composition of the quantified set is asserted, whereas in the former case its composition is presupposed. If this is indeed the case, then the notion of 'abbreviation' can be replaced by the notion of 'being more explicit': (60) is more explicit than (59) and (62) is more explicit than (61).

It is clear that interrogative quantifiers such as *who, which*, etc. correspond to the existential quantifier of the type *some*. This means that interrogative quantifiers should be represented as a disjunction and not as a conjunction. Consequently, the *wh*-question in (63) is represented by the disjunction in (64):

(63)   Which A is B?

(64)   Is it a_1 which is B or is it a_2 which is B or ... or is it a_n which is B?

Thus it is possible to reduce a *wh*-question like (63) to a disjunction of *yes-no* questions or to an alternative question with a multiple base. Since we know how to analyze *yes-no* questions and alternative questions, we know how to analyze *wh*-questions: indeed, every constituent question in (64) can be represented according to the definitional property of *yes-no* questions given in D3.2.

To represent a *wh*-question, let us specify what counts as its base. By analogy with declarative quantifiers, we will consider the unary propositional function $P(x)$ as the base of a simple *wh*-question of the form $Q \, x \, P(x)$. In this notation, P is the predicate found in the question that expresses the property which at least some members of the domain of quantification must possess. Q stands for the interrogative quantifier which binds the free variable in the propositional function $P(x)$. This quantifier can either be 'absolute' or 'restricted' depending on whether it corresponds to an interrogative pronoun like *who, what, when*, etc. or to an interrogative determiner like *which*. With these precisions in mind, we can give the following definition of a simple *wh*-question:

D3.5:   An expression E is a unary *wh*-question with base $P(x)$ iff E presupposes $P(a_1)$ or E presupposes $P(a_2)$ or ... or E presupposes $P(a_n)$.

By analogy with *yes-no* questions, the disjunction *or* in the definition above corresponds to an exclusive disjunction. Moreover, the set that is quantified over should also be exactly specified. However, I consider this not to be a problem inherent to interrogative quantifiers but a general problem that one encounters when speaking about quantifiers. For this reason I will leave it open.

Notice that we obtained representation D3.5 without applying our method of indirect interrogatives. As can be easily verified, the same result can be reached by using this method. Indeed, consider an indirect question (65) in which the *wh*-question (63) is embedded:

(65)   Bill knows which A is B.

Given the property of the verb to *know*, (65) can be decomposed into (66)

(66)   Bill knows that a_1 is B or Bill knows that a_2 is B or ... or Bill knows that a_n is B.

Since any other indirect *wh*-question in which (63) is embedded implies (66), we obtain, in conjunction with the definition of presupposition, exactly the same representation as the one given by D3.5.

A large amount of literature is devoted to a special class of *wh*-questions, the so called *multiple wh-questions*; an example is given in (67):

(67)   Who ate what?

Since, as will briefly be shown later on, these questions do not yield the same derived contents as 'simple' *wh*-questions do, I will not propose a representation for them here. Notice, however, that multiple *wh*-questions can be represented by using in the definition of the base not a unary predicate but an *n*-ary relation symbol.

The definitional property given in D3.5 yields various properties of *wh*-questions. The first property concerns the presuppositions of *wh*--questions. One can see immediately that the *wh*-question (63) presupposes (68):

(68) Some a_i's are B. (where $a_i \epsilon A$)

Indeed, according to definition D3.5, every member 'a_i is B' of the disjunction corresponding to (63) implies (68). Since every implication of a presupposition is itself a presupposition, (63) presupposes (68).

What is more interesting is the fact that definition D3.5 also implies that (69) is a presupposition of (63):

(69)   Some a_i's are not B.

This negative presupposition results from the fact that D3.5 contains an exclusive and not an inclusive disjunction: it is not true that every member of the disjunction is true at the same time.

Negative presuppositions of unary *wh*-questions have been mentioned in the literature on questions as early as 1924 (cf. Ajdukiewicz 1924). As far as I can tell, they were rarely discussed in connection with the presuppositions of questions. It seems to me, however, that negative presuppositions are as important as 'positive' ones and in some sense they constitute the essence of *wh*-questions. Thus, for (70) to carry its interrogative force of a question, both (71), the positive presupposition, and (72), the negative presupposition, must be true:

(70)   Which linguist will read this?
(71)   Some linguist will read this.
(72)   Some linguist will not read this.

Negative presuppositions of *wh*-questions are due to the presence of the *exclusive* disjunction in the representation of questions I have proposed. One might object that this disjunction, at least in the case of alternative questions and in the case of *wh*-questions, can be an *inclusive* one. In fact, as I will try to show now, in all cases we are dealing with an exclusive disjunction.

It is clear that a *yes-no* question with base S contains an exclusive disjunction: the question $Q(S)$ either presupposes S or it presupposes *not-S*; it cannot presuppose both since, in this case, we would have a contradictory presupposition. With respect to alternative questions, this reasoning does not hold since the base of an alternative question may possess members that are not necessarily mutually contradictory.

Suppose we have an alternative question $Q(S,T)$ whose base is composed of two members T and S. I suggested that such a question either presupposes S or it presupposes T but not both S *and* T. Suppose, *a contrario*, that $Q(S,T)$ also presupposes S *and* T. Given the connection which exists between indirect interrogatives and the privative opposition, this would mean that not only (73a) and (73b) are possible marked counterparts of the indirect alternative question (74), but also the conjunction of both in (73c) is a possible marked counterpart of (74):

(73)(a)   A knows that S.
    (b)   A knows that T.
    (c)   A knows that S and T.

(74)   A knows whether S or T.

According to the definition of privative opposition given in the first chapter, if a sentence Q is privatively opposed to P, where Q is the unmarked member of the opposition and P the marked one, then P intensionally asserts Q. But then, acccording to the definition of intensional assertion, *not-P* asserts *not-Q*. This would mean, if our supposition were true, that the normal negation of (73c) implies the normal negation of (74), for any sentence S and T. As such, (75) should imply (76):

(75)   A does not know that S and T.

(76)   A does not know whether S or T.

But (75) does not imply (76), even if all presuppositions are preserved. Indeed, in a situation in which (77) and (78) are true, (75) is true and (76) is false:

(77)   A knows that S.

(78)   A does not know that T.

This result is due to the fact that (73c) contains more opacity provoking material than (74), or it is possible to replace S in (73c) by an equivalent sentence S' and change the truth-value of the new sentence. But such a replacement of S by S' in (74) may not lead to a truth-value change of the new sentence thus obtained form (74).

Two additional, linguistic, arguments can be adduced to support the claim that the disjunction in the representation of questions must be an exclusive one. The first argument has to do with the fact that some particular alternative questions, which should be possible if the disjunction were inclusive, are in fact impossible; it is well-known that questions like (79) do not exist:

(79)   *Who, Bill and Joe, will go to New York?

If the disjunction in our representation of questions were inclusive, then (79) should be possible in the same way as (80) is:

(80)   Who, Bill or Joe, will go to New York?

The second linguistic argument is connected with the possible answers to an alternative question. Indeed, (81) can be easily answered by (82) or by (83), but not easily by (84):

(81)   Is Bill a mathematician or a linguist?

(82)   A linguist.

(83)   A mathematician.

(84)   A mathematician and a linguist.

The utterance in (84) is rather an answer to (85):

(85)   Is Bill a mathematician or a linguist or a mathematician *and* a linguist?

If in some cases, (84), pronounced with a special intonation, can be taken as an answer to (81), this is because (85) and (81) are semantically related and it often happens that semantically related questions yield the same answers.

A final argument for my claim is that in many languages, we do not find natural language counterparts of 'logical' disjunction in alternative questions, but a question particle.

The second property I would like to discuss briefly concerns the possible equivalence between a simple unary *wh*-question and its (verbal) negation. I have shown that, according to the representation of *yes-no* questions proposed here, there exists an equivalence between a positive and its corresponding negative *yes-no* question. The problem to which I would like to address myself now is whether there is a similar equivalence between *wh*-questions and their corresponding verbal negations; for instance, are (86) and (87) equivalent and, if they are, in what sense?

(86)   Who called?
(87)   Who did not call?

Recall first of all that negative *wh*-questions very often have a non-literal reading in which they become so-called rhetorical questions and lose their interrogative force. On this reading, they indirectly imply the negation of their positive presupposition. For instance, (87) has a positive presupposition (88) and, taken as a rhetorical question, it can express (89), the negation of (88):

(88)   Someone did not call.
(89)   Everyone called.

This rhetorical reading is due to the ambiguity of the negation which sometimes ceases to be opacity preserving and which can give rise to a double reading of both members of a privative opposition.

Suppose we are interested in the literal readings of both *wh*-questions (86) and (87). In addition, suppose that the universe of discourse or the set of quantification is in some way specified and is the same for both questions. Can we then say that there is a sense in which they are equivalent? I think that the answer depends on how we understand the interrogative pronoun *who*. The problem is the following: does (86) 'ask' to enumerate all the persons who called or is it enough to name just some but not all of them in order to answer (86) fully. In other words, do (86) and (87) mean (90) and (91), respectively:

(90)   Who exactly called?
(91)   Who exactly did not call?

It seems to me that the reading of (86) corresponding to (90) is the most natural one, but very likely another reading in which (86) 'asks' someone to name just some but not all persons who called is also possible. It is possible that in some cases and for some languages we do not get this ambiguity which in particular depends on the meaning we ascribe to the notion of *exclusive disjunction*. I have been told that some languages can mark the reading corresponding to (90) by the reduplication of the interrogative pronoun or by other non-lexical devices. If this is indeed the case, then we can show that for such marked readings there is an equivalence between (86) and (87). This equivalence results from our representation of questions by considering the corresponding multiple disjunctions and keeping in mind the fact that, among the possible disjuncts occurring in these disjunctions, there are positive and negative ones and that these cannot both have the same truth-value.

Before making some general comments about the idea of a question underlying the above results, I would like to say a few words about various types of questions. The classification of questions was not my main concern in this chapter. I accepted a natural classification with which many researchers in the field of erotetic logic agree (cf. Wunderlich 1981) by distinguishing only three types of questions: *yes-no*, alternative, and *wh*-questions. Logicians distinguish, and sometimes discuss, many other types of questions (cf. Kubinski 1971; Harrah n.d.). It seems to me, however, that not all logically possible questions are realized in natural language. What types of questions can be constructed in natural language is an empirical question which cannot be solved in isolation, without taking into account other related phenomena. We know, for instance, that there is a relation between what constituents can be 'questioned' and what constituents can be focused on. Now, interestingly enough, not all logically possible constituents can in reality be focused on or emphasized. The reasons for such restrictions are far from evident, but clearly, they are related to the possibility of forming special questions. So an exhaustive and adequate classification of questions must await the solution of other, more general problems.

There is a special subclass of *wh*-questions, the so-called multiple *wh*-questions, whose existence I have mentioned but which I have not discussed. Multiple *wh*-questions apparently do not have an upper limit on the number of interrogative noun phrases which can occur in them. Compare the following questions:

(92)   Which linguists wrote which books?

(93)   Which linguists wrote which books on what subject?

(94)   Which linguists wrote which books on what subject for what reason?

I must say that I have various problems with multiple *wh*-questions. First of all I am unable, even in my native language to freely construct many multiple *wh*-questions in the way the above examples would suggest. Furthermore, I have serious problems in understanding what exactly multiple *wh*-questions ask. I tend to consider them as 'echo-questions'. I some cases, I think I am able to understand multiple *wh*-questions, but only by ascribing some special presuppositions to them. For instance, it seems to me that (92) presupposes (95) and that (96) presupposes (97):

(95)   Every linguist wrote some book.
(96)   Who ate what?
(97)   Everybody ate something.

Such presuppositions, as far as I can see, cannot be easily obtained by the mechanism I have proposed. Furthermore, multiple *wh*-questions seem to differ from 'simple' *wh*-questions in the readings that can be derived from both types of questions. According to my competence, at least with respect to those multiple questions that I can grasp, only simple *wh*-questions permit rhetorical readings. As far as I can judge, there are no multiple 'rhetorical questions'.

Although the difficulties with multiple questions I have just mentioned may have a subjective basis, there are more objective reasons for these difficulties that go back to the nature and structure of natural language. It is quite possible that the asymmetry between the subject NP and the object NP in natural language entails the asymmetry in the semantic roles played by the corresponding interrogative NP's. Similarly, the fact that there seems to be a limit on the number of emphasized constituents in a sentence may entail the limitation in the number of interrogative noun phrases occurring in a multiple *wh*-question. But again, all this requires independent and general research.

I am now in a position to comment on the main result of this chapter, which is the picture of questions that emerges from the various representations of questions I have proposed. In my comments I will restrict myself to *yes-no* questions, which represent, as we have seen, a basic type of questions; all other types of questions can be analyzed with the help of *yes-no* questions or at least with the help of the methods used to analyze *yes-no* questions.

According to the description proposed here, a *yes-no* question is an expression of the sentence category such that it has two possible mutually exclusive presuppositions (cf. D3.2) which are given in the form of an exclusive disjunction of presuppositions. As I already pointed out, the fact that a question is a disjunction of presuppositions and not a disjunction of assertions or statements distinguishes my proposal from other proposals in which the (exclusive) disjunction plays an essential role. In those other approaches (for instance, Harrah (1961, 1963)), an interrogative sentence is taken to be synonymous with a declarative sentence, which is an exclusive disjunction whose disjuncts are the direct answers (the members of the base).

Furthermore, we can say that, in some sense, maximal presuppositions of a question are not fixed *a priori*, 'analytically' so to speak. In opposition to other sentences, presuppositions of interrogative sentences cannot be fully determined on the basis of the sentence form alone; world knowledge is necessary to determine in a unique way the presuppositions of an interrogative sentence. This indetermination of presuppositions, their possible variation, explains why a question is semantically incomplete and needs to be completed: this constitutes the interrogative force of a question and it is the basic reason for the fact that a question 'asks' something. When an answer to the question is given, it ceases to be incomplete because its presuppositions become 'fixed'.

When we look at the various members of a definitional disjunction, we notice that they correspond to possible direct answers to the question of which the disjunction is the representation. This means that, according to my proposal, a question presupposes its possible direct answers. Now, since an answer presupposes the corresponding question — because answers are answers to *questions* — we can say that a question, according to my description, *presupposes* its proper interrogative force. This fact is in agreement with the result I have tried to justify in the preceding chapter by somewhat different methods and it gives, it seems to me, an additional justification for my proposal.

Finally, the analysis I have proposed leads to an interesting 'pragmatic' property of questions: questions, as described above, presuppose the existence of a person who can ask the question and of the person who can answer the question. More precisely, the existence of the question expressed by (98) entails (99) and (100):

(98) $Q(S)$.

(99)   Someone does not know whether S or not.

(100)   Someone knows whether S or not.

Suppose, *a contrario*, that (101), the description of the question $Q(S)$, is true but (99) is false:

(101) $Q(S)$ maximally presupposes S or it maximally presupposes *not-S*.

If (99) is false then (102) is true:

(102)   Everyone knows that S or everyone knows that *not-S*.

Since every indirect question which takes the question $Q(S)$ as complement implies either (99) or (100), if our supposition were true, the question (98) would presuppose (102). But this would mean that (101) is false since neither S nor *not-S* would be *maximally* presupposed; the maximal presupposition would correspond to one of the disjuncts of (102). The second part of my claim, i.e. the claim that if (98) exists then (100) is true, can be proved analogously.

Sentence (99) can be interpreted as stating that there is someone who does not know the truth value of the sentence S. So this person is entitled to ask a question about the truth-value of S. Sentence (100), on the other hand, states that there is someone who knows the truth-value of S. Hence this person can answer the question (98). Consequently, the existence of (98) entails the existence of someone who may ask that question and of someone who can answer it.

A similar reasoning applies to other types of questions: when there is a question there is always someone who may ask it and someone who can answer it. Consequently, given the other general properties I have discussed, the description of questions proposed here explains the *raison d'être* of questions and shows why interrogative sentences *ask* questions even if they do not explicitly contain the verb 'to ask'.

4. NON-DECLARATIVES

Although all the preceding chapters are devoted to non-declarative sentences, no attempt has thus far been made to define them or at least to give a general description of them. This will be done in the present chapter: using the tool of opaque operators, I will propose a general syntactico-semantic characterization of all types of non-declarative sentences. I will also show that there are precisely three main types of non-declaratives which I will traditionally call interrogatives, imperatives, and exclamations.

For a long time, grammarians have been trying to devise various systems which would enable them to classify all the types of sentences one finds in natural languages. The most recent and probably the most complete attempt is that of generative linguists and philosophers of language working in the Austinian spirit. This is the so-called *performative approach*. First of all, I would like to present some objections to this approach.

One of the objections has already been mentioned in connection with questions and explicit performative sentences. I have shown that illocutionary forces associated with non-declarative sentences and forces induced by explicit performative verbs are not semantically equivalent: the former constitute the presupposed semantic content, whereas the latter correspond to the asserted content. Evidently, this objection is not only valid for interrogative sentences.

My second criticism has to do with the quantitative difference between performative sentences and formally marked non-declarative sentences. More precisely, it concerns the numerical difference between performative verbs and types of known non-declarative sentences. In a theory calling for the dominance of performative verbs, one meets with two difficulties when one tries to give a homogeneous interpretation of different illocutionary forces. First of all, it is often not an easy task to determine which performative verb should be associated with which grammatically given illocutionary force. For instance, we do not know what performative verb, if any, corresponds to the exclamatory force. This is indeed very surprising because, and here we meet with the second difficulty, performative verbs so glaringly outnumber the types of grammatically marked sentences that one can wonder whether one should pay so much attention to the rather fortuitous correspondences sometimes found between performative verbs and grammatical markers. In other words, the acceptance of the performative approach forces us to privilege a very restricted number of performatives and oppose them in a very arbitrary way to a very large number of remaining performatives.

The existence of a relation between illocutionary forces induced by performative verbs and forces induced grammatically would be interesting if we could show that they can be mutually defined. Thus it would be significant if the combination of grammatically induced forces with other semantically and pragmatically essential elements could permit the definition of any illocutionary force induced by a performative verb.

Let me give two examples, First, take a typical performative verb such as *to promise*:

(1)   I promise to stop tickling you.

It is possible to understand the promise expressed by a performative sentence as an 'order' given to oneself. Then (1) would be 'equivalent' to a direct order given in (2):

(2)   Let me stop tickling you!
         (I order me to stop tickling you.)

The other example involves the illocutionary force proper to the performative verb *to forbid*. A prohibition or an interdiction or a forbidding can be defined as a 'negative order'. Thus (3) is conceptually equivalent to (4):

(3)   I forbid you to swim here.
(4)   Don't swim here!

In some languages, however, the two illocutionary forces which were defined in the examples above by means of more 'simple' ones may be expressed directly by grammatical means: there are morphemes expressing prohibition (in Mongolian and in Chinese, for instance), and there are languages which have a morpheme indicating a promise or rather a firm intention (Gilyak, for instance). This means that some illocutionary forces which are 'complex' in one language are 'simple' in another language. Thus, once again, the supposed correlation between grammatical markers of illocutionary forces and performative verbs appears to be highly arbitrary. This arbitrariness becomes even more evident if we realize that many sentences of a grammatically marked type are in fact ambiguous from the point of view of the illocutionary force they can carry: (4), for instance, can be considered also as an advice.

Given the above difficulties with the performative approach, I will take into consideration possible formal markers and not the presence or absence of a particular performative verb when speaking about non-declarative sentences. In fact, performative sentences with performative use will be considered as declarative sentences.

In approaching the problem of the general characterization of non-declarative sentences, I will proceed as follows. First, I will show that it is not possible to find purely formal, i.e. syntactic and/or morphological, criteria distinguishing various types of non-declarative sentences. Then, I will show how the method of complex opaque sentences, which was introduced to define presuppositions and to analyze indirect non-declaratives, can be used to explain why the number of sentence types is so limited. Finally, I will show how this limitation in number can be correlated with some purely semantic phenomena

To begin with, I would like to underline that my analysis will be concerned with *sentences*, i.e. expressions which contain a verb phrase and in principle an argument of that verb phrase. Thus I will exclude from my description non-sentential expressions like the following ones:

(5)   Down with telepathy!
(6)   Never mind.
(7)   Oh, the naughty girl!

On the other hand, I will include expressions which, although they do not explicitly contain the argument of the verb phrase, can easily be completed by such an argument. This is particularly the case of imperative sentences, where very often the missing subject NP can be added. Thus we can have subjectless imperatives like (8) as well as imperatives with an overt subject NP like (9) and (10):

(8)   Close the door!
(9)   You close the door.
(10)   Everyone stay in the room!

I think that the situation with imperative sentences is similar to that with declarative sentences in languages where the subject noun phrase need not be present on the surface.

I have described the opposition between non-declarative sentences and declarative ones in terms of the presence of a formal mark attached to the former sentences and its absence from the latter ones. These formal marks are in fact sentence mood indicators, and they can take one of the following forms: special intonation, interrogative words, special deictic words, indicators of verbal mood, differences in word order, affixes and particles, ellipsis of the subject, exclamatory words, special performative adverbs, etc. It is clear that the formal marks do not really serve to distinguish declaratives from non-declaratives but rather to mark special moods and, in general, it is impossible to distinguish between 'declarative moods' and 'non-declarative' ones. In addition, there is an interdependence between declarative and non-declarative moods. For instance, there is a close relation between tense and aspect markers on the one hand and order markers on the other hand: past orders hardly exist, and in many languages negative orders are incompatible with the perfective aspect. Thus there cannot be a purely grammatical basis for the distinction between declaratives and non-declaratives.

In the logical approach, declarative sentences are usually distinguished from non-declarative ones by the possibility of having a truth-value or not: only declarative sentences are supposed to have one of the two truth-values. Although this criterion provides an abstract characterization of declaratives, is of no practical use. Given, however, a general correspondence between linguistic forms and their semantic content, or between syntax and semantics, one can rightly ask whether the semantic truth-value criterion cannot be replaced by a corresponding syntactic one.

Since there is a relationship between the syntactic operation of negation (of negating) and truth-values, one could be led to think that the syntactic negation could provide us with the required test. But this is far from evident for the following reasons. Some, but not all types of non-declaratives, admit the syntactic operation of negation; thus we can negate imperative and interrogative sentences:

(11)(a) Drink this!
    (b) Don't drink this!

    (a) Is he bright?
    (b) Is he not bright?

Exclamative sentences on the other hand cannot be negated:

(13)(a) How clever he is!
    (b)*How clever he is not.

Moreover, there are many declarative sentences which cannot be negated either. Take, for instance, sentences containing the well-known *positive polarity items*:

(14)(a) She is rather stupid.
    (b)*She is not rather stupid.

(15)(a) He has already written his letter.

(b)*He has not already written his letter.

Another group of declarative sentences which cannot be negated easily consists of complex declarative sentences containing various 'non-logical' connectives. For instance, it is difficult to imagine what negations would correspond to complex sentences containing the conjunctions *but* or *although*:

(16)(a) Bill arrived late but without his sister.

(b)?It is not true that Bill arrived late but without his sister.

(17)(a) She left early although she was not tired.

(b)?It is not true that she left although she was not tired.

Thus we are faced with the following situation: some clearly non-declarative sentences can be negated whereas others cannot. Similarly, some declarative sentences allow negation and others do not. This shows, it seems to me, that negation cannot serve as the criterion for the distinction between declarative and non-declarative sentences.

Let us now try another possibility. Suppose that we define declarative sentences as those sentences that may be subject to the interrogative transformation or, in semantic terms, as those which can serve as a base for a *yes-no* question. This proposal could be justified in the following way: since declarative sentences bear truth-values they can almost directly be used as possible answers to *yes-no* questions. Then a true declarative sentence would be a true answer to the corresponding question and a false sentence would be considered as a false answer. But, in this case, we meet with the same type of difficulties as those we met with in the case of negation. In particular, declarative sentences which do not admit negation cannot easily serve as a base for a *yes-no* question.

(18)   ?Isn't she rather stupid?

(19)   *Did Bill arrive but without his sister?

(20)   *Did she leave early although she was not tired?

Notice that the interrogative transformation does not always behave in the way the negative transformation does. For instance, it is possible to derive a *yes-no* question from the declarative base (15a):

(21)   Has he already written his letter?

These facts also force us to give up the tests of interrogation and of the *yes-no* question.

Up to now, I have considered interrogatives and imperatives as two distinct types of non-declarative sentences. Now I would like to show briefly that one type cannot be reduced to the other except in a very *ad hoc* way.

General principles of logic always permit the reduction of a number of different categories. Such a reduction is usually very artificial since it is based on the very abstract principles of abstraction from essential properties. We have already seen some attempts to reduce questions to orders: a question would be an order applying not to a 'physical' action but to a linguistic act or to a linguistic action; a question would be an order to say something, in particular to give a verbal answer to a question.

There is however another possible relationship between questions and orders: an order can be understood as an answer to very special questions like the ones given in (22), (23), or (24):

(22)   What should I do?
(23)   What should we do?
(24)   How should I do it?

One notices indeed that most imperative sentences can be properly considered as answers to one of these questions.

Concerning the first analogy, i.e. that a question is a special order applied to a linguistic act, it is not at all evident that questions directly carry such an order; as I have tried to show in the preceding chapter, the fact that one wants to answer a question is not an essential feature of a question, from a semantic point of view. This rather pragmatic property of questions follows from an indirect meaning derivation based on the fact that questions are 'presuppositionally' incomplete. It is thus by accident, so to speak, that we answer a question when we complete or fix its presuppositions. From this point of view, a 'normal' question differs from asking or requesting something directly, with the help of lexical means available through the existence of explicit performative sentences.

The second possible relationship between questions and orders, i.e. the fact that orders are in some sense answers to some type of questions, does not provide a sufficient basis for the identification of the two types of non-declaratives. Indeed, the questions (22)-(24) are very special ones, in particular because they contain first person pronouns. Moreover, their bases contain modals like *shall* or *should*, and consequently, they suppose a kind of pre-existent, continuous obligation which is different from the obligation imposed by orders. Orders create temporal 'non-generic' obligations which are thus different in nature from modal obligations.

Notice in connection with the last remark that the 'literal' answers to questions like (22), (23), or (24) are not exactly imperative sentences but rather 'modal' sentences of the type (25) or (26):

(25)   You should leave by this evening.

(26)   We should write this letter.

Finally notice that the grammatical markers of interrogative and imperative sentences are usually quite different.

It seems to me that, given the above facts, we cannot simply consider questions as special orders. Later on, I will show what the essential semantic difference between them is. What is the status of exclamative sentences in this context? How do they differ from interrogative sentences?

We have already seen that exclamations, as opposed to other non-declaratives, contain verb phrases which do not admit syntactic negation. There are, however, many other differences. First of all, the number of constituents from which exclamative sentences can be 'formed' is very restricted. In particular, it is impossible to construct an exclamative sentence 'based' on subject and object NP's or on time or place adverbs. In other words, exclamations cannot be introduced by *who, what, when* and *where*:

(27)(a) What did you see?

(b)*What Bill saw!

(28)(a) When did he call?

(b)*When Bill called!

None of these sentences can be interpreted as expressing an exclamation. Furthermore, if an interrogative sentence and an exclamative sentence can both be introduced by the same interrogative modifier, then other formal marks must be different. For instance, in English the word order for interrogatives and for exclamations is not the same:

(29)(a) How tall is Bill?

(b) How tall Bill is!

(30)(a) How fast can Bill drive?

(b) How fast Bill can drive!

These facts also force us not to identify the class of interrogatives with the class of exclamations.

We can now begin to look for common features of all types of non-declaratives in order to characterize them in a general way. We can start by recalling that all types have corresponding indirect non-declaratives: (31a) is an indirect

question corresponding to the direct question (31b), (32a) is an indirect imperative whose direct counterpart is given in (32b), and in (33) we find indirect and
direct exclamatives respectively:

(31)(a) Bill forgot who called.
    (b) Who called?

(32)(a) Stop smoking!
    (b) I want you to stop smoking.

(33)(a) I am surprised at how stupid he is!
    (b) How stupid he is!

We know already that indirect non-declaratives are opaque sentences, i.e. sentences constructed with normally opaque operators. We also know that not only
question taking operators are normally opaque ones. So now we can ask ourselves whether there are other, non-opaque operators which can take non-
declarative sentences as arguments. And surprisingly enough, the answer is no:
only opaque operators can take non-declarative complements. The classical
extensional sentential operators such as *It is true* or *It is false* cannot collocate
with non-declaratives, as the following examples show:

(34)   *It is true that everyone stop drinking.
(35)   *It is true how sure to win Bill is.
(36)   *It is false whether it will rain or not.
(37)   *It is absolutely false how easily persuaded to leave the country Bill was.
(38)   *It is false whom did you see.

Extensional operators are not the only ones which cannot take non-declarative complements. Also opaque, but not normally opaque, sentential operators
represented by the classical modal operators cannot collocate with non-declarative complements:

(39)   *It is necessary whether he is an idiot.
(40)   *It is possible what a beautiful house he has.
(41)   *It is necessary that everybody stay quiet.

The restriction illustrated by these examples can be presented in a more general
fashion as follows. First of all, notice that non-normally opaque operators can
take only a *that*-complementizer: sentences containing the following expressions
are impossible: *It is true how, *It is possible whether, *It is necessary if, etc.
Furthermore, in English, non-declarative sentences cannot be introduced by a
that-complementizer. Consequently, non-declarative sentences cannot be

embedded in non-normally opaque operators.

An interesting situation can be found in French. The French complementizer *que* roughly corresponds to the English *that*. In French, however, many non-declarative sentences can be introduced by *que*:

(42) *Qu'est-ce que tu veux?*
      What do you want?

(43) *Qu'elle ferme la porte!*
      Let her close the door!

(44) *Que ce livre est beau!*
      What a beautiful book this is!

In (42) we have a question, in (43) an order, and in (44) an exclamation. A question cannot be embedded in non-normally opaque operators:

(45) **Il est faux qu'est-ce que tu veux?*
      It is false what do you want?

(46) **Il est nécessaire qu'est-ce que tu veux?*
      It is necessary what do you want?

One notices, however, that imperatives and exclamatives can be embedded in at least some non-normally opaque operators:

(47) *Jacques a fait en sorte qu'elle ferme la porte.*
      Jacques made it in the way that she closes the door.

(48) *Il est faux qu'elle ferme la porte.*
(49) *Il est probable que ce livre est beau.*
(50) *Il n'est pas vrai que ce livre est beau.*

An interesting fact is that (47)-(50) can in no way be considered as indirect non-declaratives. For instance, (47) and (48) neither directly nor indirectly express an order. Similarly, (49) and (50) do not express the exclamation which is expressed by (44), their complement sentence.

Now, declarative sentences can usually be embedded in non-normally opaque operators:

(51) It is possible that he arrived but without his sister.
(52) It is not necessary that it rains.

We thus arrive at the following characterization of non-declarative sentences: they are sentences that can only be embedded in normally opaque operators without losing their essential semantical property. It follows from this definition that indirect non-declarative sentences can only be opaque sentences. On the other hand, as we have seen, indirect declaratives can be non-opaque sentences.

The above characterization of non-declarative sentences permits us to prove the following property of non-declaratives:

(53)   Non-declarative sentences do not declare anything.

Recall that a sentence S declares a sentence T iff (a) S and T have a common argument which can detect the opacity of the normally opaque operator in which S or T can be embedded, (b) T is formally no more complex than S, and (c) there is a complex sentence which contains S as its argument and which asserts T. Suppose, *a contrario*, that a non-declarative sentence S declares the sentence T. Then, according to the above definition, there exists a complex sentence $O(S)$ which asserts T. So $O(S)$ implies T without presupposing T. But since $O(S)$ and T are opaquely related because S and T have a common opacity detecting argument (according to clause (a) of the definition of declaration) and since O is a normally opaque operator because only opaque sentences contain non-declarative sentences, $O(S)$ must presuppose T (according to property P1′ which is the generalization of property P1). But a sentence cannot possibly presuppose and assert another sentence at the same time. Consequently (53) is true.

Now, we already know that declarative sentences do have declarations. In particular, they declare themselves because, for any declarative sentence S, there exists a complex sentence *It is true that* S which asserts S. Declarative non-analytic sentences can also declare other sentences which are syntactically less complex than the declaring sentences. Thus a conjunction of two non-analytic sentences declares each of its conjuncts. Furthermore, declarative non-analytic sentences also assert something; in particular, they assert themselves but they can also assert syntactically more complex sentences. Thus (54) asserts (55):

(54)   Bill arrived.
(55)   Bill arrived or Sue called.

Of course, declarative analytic sentences, i.e. declarative sentences which presuppose every sentence syntactically simpler than themselves, declare only themselves and they do not assert anything syntactically simpler than themselves.

It follows from the above description that the only intensional semantic relation into which non-declarative sentences can enter is the presupposition relation. In the preceding chapter, I proposed to analyze questions as expressions which either presuppose their declarative base or the negation of their base. So now, we are entitled to ask whether other types of non-declaratives enter into a presupposition relation with their declarative base. For exclamative sentences this relation is rather simple: they presuppose their declarative base. Thus (56a) presupposes (56b) and (57a) presupposes (57b):

(56)(a) How sure to win Bill was!
    (b) Bill was sure to win.

(57)(a) How quickly Mami can run!
    (b) Mami can run quickly.[9]

Indeed, the definition of presupposition says that a non-declarative sentence S presupposes a (declarative) sentence T if any indirect non-declarative sentence containing S as its argument entails T. Now, Elliot (1974) and Grimshaw (1979) have noticed that only factive predicates take exclamative sentences as complements. This can be illustrated by the following set of examples:

(58)   It's amazing how quickly Mami can run.
(59)   Sue realized how stupidly Bill was behaving.
(60)   I found out how sure to win Bill was.
(61)   It's amazing what a big nose he has.
(62)   It is not surprising that he has such a big nose.

If this generalization is true, then given the property of factive predicates one can easily understand that exclamative sentences presuppose their declarative base.

How can we determine the presuppositions of imperative sentences? Since the syntax of direct and indirect imperatives is more complicated than the syntax of other non-declaratives, and especially, since imperative sentences can express a great variety of orders, it is necessary to specify the type of orders that will be primarily analyzed.

Among the different types of orders, there is one which seems to me more basic than others: what I have in mind are the so-called *orders to be immediately obeyed.* These are orders issued in the presence of the person to which they are addressed, *viz.* the addressee, and they require immediate obedience. Concerning their linguistic form, one notices that they do not contain time adverbials except maybe redundant deictic adverbs like *now, right now, immediately*, etc. Thus (63) is an example of such a simple order I have in mind:

(63)   Close the door!

I consider this order as equivalent to (64) and it seems to me that (63) cannot mean for instance (65):

(64)   Close the door (just) now!

(65)   Close the door tomorrow evening!

The presence of the adverbial *tomorrow evening* in (65) entails, it seems to me, that the obligation created by (65) is in some sense weaker and less absolute than the obligation created by (63). This obligation is weaker because its validity is subject to the satisfaction of more conditions than the validity of the obligation expressed by (63). In other words, much more things can happen which can delay or cancel the obligations between now and tomorrow evening than between now and immediately after. This means that orders like (65), which are orders not to be immediately obeyed, are 'implicitly conditional' orders: there are many undetermined implicit 'ifs' whose truth is assumed when (65) is taken to express a command or an order; (65) in fact means something like (66):

(66)   Close the door tomorrow evening, if the house is not burnt, if the door is not stolen, if you are not dead, etc.

The basic orders, being the orders to be immediately obeyed, do not suppose the truth of implicit conditions that differ from the 'normal' presuppositions of imperatives.

Another aspect of imperatives which needs some clarification before approaching the problem of presuppositions concerns the base of imperative sentences. I have already mentioned the difficulty with the underlying subject of imperatives, and I will not discuss it further. Similar problems exist, it seems to me, with the underlying tense of imperatives: given the surface form of an imperative sentence, it is practically impossible to associate a particular tense, if any, with the verbal form used and, correspondingly, the time of 'actions' concerned. The solution to this problem depends, of course, on the type of order we are interested in, but if we restrict ourselves to basic orders, i.e. orders to be immediately obeyed, it is quite natural to assume that it is the present continuous tense which underlies them. Indeed, we know that only sentences with active verbs may be subject to the imperative creating transformation. But active sentences are at the same time sentences whose verbs can be put into a continuous tense. This means that the imperative and the continuous tense are correlated, and I will further explicitate this correlation by postulating that the continuous tense underlies imperative constructions, at least those which express immediate orders.

According to what I have just said, the imperative sentence (67), taken as a basic order, has (68) as its base:

(67)   Leave!
(68)   You are leaving.

It might be possible to avoid pragmatic connotations induced by the second person in (68) and consider orders in a somewhat more abstract way; since an action is important for an order and not necessarily the author of the action, one could omit the author and mention only the action. Then we would get 'logical' or 'non-pragmatic' orders like (69) with a base such as (70):

(69)   Let the book be closed!
(70)   The book is being closed.

Such 'logical' imperatives would operate only on nominalizations and the actions associated with them: an order would call for the existence of an action, and its base would assert the existence of that action. Then, in fact, the purely logical form of (69) would be (71) and its corresponding base would be something like (72):

(71)   Let there exist the action of closing the book.
(72)   There exists the action of closing the book.

Such a non-pragmatic approach to imperatives would come closer in spirit to the analysis of questions made in the preceding chapter and to the general tendency of this book. It would have the advantage of avoiding the analysis of the complicated contribution of various pragmatic elements, and it would lead to a better understanding of the purely 'logical' mechanism of ordering. I will not, however, work with logical examples such as (69)-(72), as I consider them not natural enough, and will continue my analysis with pragmatically charged examples like (67) or (68).*

We can now turn back to the problem of the presuppositions of imperative sentences. It seems to me that basic imperative sentences presuppose the negation of their base: (73a) presupposes (73b) and (74a) presupposes (74b):

(73)(a) Drive slowly!
    (b) You are not driving slowly.

(74)(a) Shut the second window!
    (b) You are not shutting the second window.

To show that we do get the presuppositions indicated, we should apply our generalized definition of presupposition. Since we are dealing with non-declarative sentences, we should consider all corresponding indirect non-declaratives, i.e. indirect imperatives. The following sentences represent a sample of the indirect imperatives required:

(75)   Bill wants you to drive slowly.
(76)   Sue would like you to drive slowly.
(77)   I wish you to drive slowly.

In my opinion, all these sentences, irrespective of their subject NP's, imply (73b). If this is really so, (73a), the complement sentence of all these indirect imperatives, presupposes (73b).

One important thing should be noted in connection with the indirect imperatives (75)-(77): their constituent operators are not sentential operators, although they are clearly opaque operators. This means that not all the results established in the first chapter and concerning sentential opaque operators can be applied directly to the above sentences. In particular, the above examples in no way contradict property P5, which states that there are no negative factives, i.e. opaque sentences which imply the negation of their complement sentence: the base of (73a) is not the complement of (75), (76), or (77).

Moreover, the negation of an indirect imperative is no longer an indirect imperative, but becomes the indirect negated imperative. Thus the negation of (75), which is at least on one reading equivalent to (78), should be considered as an indirect negative imperative, i.e. an indirect imperative corresponding to (79), the 'verbal' negation of the positive imperative (73a):

(78)   Bill does not want you to drive slowly.
(79)   Don't drive slowly!

Hence neither property P1 (if $O(P)$ implies P then $not\text{-}O(P)$ also implies P) nor its generalization P1´ are applicable to indirect imperatives.

Finally, notice that the fact that indirect imperatives have non-sentential (reduced) complements is closely related to the possibility of omitting the subject of imperatives and to the non-existence of 'first person' imperatives.

We are now in a position to define exclamations and imperatives:

D4.1:   A non-declarative sentence $E(S)$ is an exclamative sentence with base S iff $E(S)$ maximally presupposes S.

For imperative sentences the definition is quite analogous:

D4.2:   A non-declarative sentence $I(S)$ is an imperative sentence with base S iff $I(S)$ maximally presupposes $non\text{-}S$.

Given the results of the preceding chapter, we can also define a *yes-no* question in the following way:

D4.3:   A non-declarative sentence $Q(S)$ is an interrogative sentence with base S iff $Q(S)$ maximally presupposes S or $Q(S)$ maximally presupposes *non-S*.

Before making some general comments on these definitions, I would like to show how their application can solve a particular problem in French. Some non-declarative sentences in French are ambiguous and can be interpreted as exclamations or as orders. This is the case with (80):

(80)   *Qu'il marche rapidement!*

This sentence can be translated either by (81) or by (82):

(81)   How rapidly he walks (he is walking)!

(82)   Let him walk rapidly!

The base of (80) can be either true or false. According to definitions D4.1 and D4.2, if the base of (80) is true then it expresses an exclamation and should be translated as (81), and if the base is false then (80) expresses an order and should be translated as (82).

Let me summarize the main results of this chapter and make some general comments on them. After I showed that it is difficult, if not impossible, to define non-declarative sentences in formal non-semantic terms, I proposed to consider as non-declarative sentences those sentences which can be embedded in opaque operators only. From this, it follows that non-declarative sentences do not declare anything, and that the only semantic relation they can enter into with their bases is the presupposition relation. In my opinion, the fact that non-declaratives do not declare anything can be considered as the linguistic counterpart of the logician's claim that non-declaratives lack a truth-value. Showing the equivalence, however, between these two characterizations may not appear to be straightforwardly possible since the two claims are formulated in different 'metalanguages'.

Subsequently, I have shown that the two non-declarative types, exclamations and imperatives, can be characterized in the following way: exclamative sentences are non-declaratives which maximally presuppose their base, and imperative sentences are non-declaratives which maximally presuppose the negation of their base. In the preceding chapter, I have shown that interrogatives are non-declaratives that either maximally presuppose their base or that maximally presuppose the negation of their base. Now, given a declarative sentence S, three non-trivial boolean operations are possible on S: the assertion of S, the negation of S, and the disjunction of S and its negation. The fourth possibility, the conjunction of

S and its negation can be excluded as it gives a trivial result, *viz.* the logical contradiction. Since the three types of non-declaratives are correlated with the three non-trivial operations on the base, and since there are no other 'interesting' combinations of the base, it follows from the above description of non-declaratives that there are only three types of non-declaratives having a one-member base.

Grammarians have traditionally assumed that in fact there are more than three different types of moods. In a recent study, Zaefferer (1983) compared six typologically quite different languages (English, German, Guarani, Quechua, Chinese, and Korean), and established that they all display the following structurally marked illocution types:

(a)   assertive (declarative);

(b)   erotetic (interrogative);

(c)   directive (jussive/imperative);

(d)   subassertive (dubitative); and

(e)   a-expressive (expressing amazement, exclamatory).

In addition, some, but not all languages have the following illocution types:

(f)   w-expressive (expressing a wish, optative);

(g)   we-directive (propositive);

(h)   reporting assertive (quotative);

(i)   pseudo-erotetic (rhetorical interrogative); and

(j)   commissive (promissive).

It is far from evident that, except for the first assertive one, all these structurally marked illocution types (i.e. marked by a set of syntactic features which uniquely determines the illocution type) should correspond to one of the non-declarative types in that they do not have a truth-value. In fact, most of the illocution types mentioned by Zaefferer are assertive subtypes. This seems to be the case with the subassertive (dubitative), we-directive (propositive), reporting assertive, and optative. Furthermore, the pseudo-erotetic and commissive types are also just subtypes of some other 'classical' types. In other words, all the types above should be considered rather as mood types, and moreover, they are reducible to just four, including the declarative sentence type, that I have been discussing.

It can be claimed that my proposal does not exclude the possible existence of special subtypes among the four types I have distinguished, namely one declarative and three non-declarative. In fact, we have seen that these types can be subdivided when discussing imperative sentences. I have restricted myself to basic imperatives, i.e. imperatives expressing orders to be immediately obeyed. I have pointed out that these are orders without any implicit condition of obedience; most orders implying the obligation for the future have various undetermined implicit conditions for compliance. These conditions depend on the type of verb used, its aspectual content, the accompanying adverbials, etc. In addition, we can have generic orders or commands, in quite the same way as we can have generic or non-generic statements.

Moreover, the three non-declarative types I have distinguished are characterized by the fact that they have only one base or, alternatively, by the fact that their corresponding *indirect* non-declaratives are constructed from *unary* opaque operators. I have left open the possibility of non-declaratives with two, or theoretically more than two, bases. In this case, the corresponding indirect non-declaratives would be constructed from *binary* or, generally, *n*-ary opaque operators. A good candidate for such a 'binary' non-declarative sentence seems to me the French 'optative' sentence given in (83):

(83)   *Si on allait au cinema.*
        Let us go to the movies — why not go to the movies.

The form of this sentence clearly indicates that it is based on or that it 'derives' from a conditional which usually has two different members. In addition, at least some conditionals are good candidates for a binary non-truth-functional sentential operator. Since intensional binary operators have not been studied to date, I feel that it is quite justified to omit the analysis of binary non-declaratives in this work.

I would not like to give the impression that I am not aware of one important shortcoming of the analysis of non-declaratives proposed in this chapter: it concerns the notion of the base of a non-declarative sentence. Although, intuitively, the notion of a base is clear, its precise definition is not without difficulties, I will mention just two of them.

First, some non-declaratives are possible even if their base is not possible, at least in a positive form. Thus we can have a question like (84) but its 'corresponding' base (85) is not acceptable because of the presence of a polarity item:

(84)   Has anybody a pencil?
(85)   *Anybody has a pencil.

This problem could be solved by transforming an impossible sequence into a possible one without essentially changing the semantic aspect of the sentence. Also, one could postulate negative bases or bases without polarity items in them.

Any such move, however, is only possible if we know exactly what the semantic contributions of polarity items are, how sentences with polarity items relate to sentences without them, etc. I think that none of these problems really has a general solution.

The second difficulty we meet with when using the notion of a base has to do with its relative syntactic complexity. Intuitively, when we say that a non-declarative sentence has a base S, we suppose *inter alia* that the non-declarative sentence is syntactically derived from S. This entails that S is syntactically or formally simpler than the corresponding non-declarative. And this is generally true except for imperative sentences: we have seen that their base is in some way more complex than the imperatives themselves. In fact, this situation is found not only in English: Wachtel (1979) examined about seventeen languages, some related to each other, some very distinct, and showed rather convincingly that the bare verbal stem is used as an imperative in most of these languages. Of course, the fact that, intuitively, a bare stem is simpler than a finite form does not mean that it is always like that: before defining an operational notion of complexity, we must determine the measure of complexity. It is theoretically possible that on one measure the construction C is more complex than the construction C', whereas on the other measure we get the opposite result. This means, at any rate, that we are in need of a clarification of some basic notions used in the above analysis.

Were the notion of a base precise enough, we would be able to answer various questions concerning the possible equivalence or mutual dependence of the proposed concepts, thus making the proposed analysis more complete. In particular, an interesting question is whether it is sufficient just to maximally presuppose the base (or a less complex declarative sentence) in order to be a non-declarative sentence with the given base. In other words, would it not be possible to simplify definitions D4.1-D4.3 by omitting the clause that imperatives, exclamations, and interrogatives are non-declarative sentences.

More precisely, suppose that our notion of the base of a non-declarative sentence is precise enough to answer whether (86) is true:

(86)   If a sentence E maximally presupposes a 'non-trivial' boolean combination of a less complex, syntactically related sentence S then E is a non-declarative sentence with base S.

Clearly, if (86) is true (given a precise interpretation of all the concepts involved) then definitions D4.1-D4.3 can be simplified. Furthermore, if (86) is true other characterizations of non-declaratives can be obtained. For the moment, however, this cannot be done.

The above technical difficulties cannot keep me from making some perhaps highly speculative remarks on the semantic impact of my proposal. In the chapter on questions (chapter 3), I suggested that, on this 'non-lexical' approach to non-declarative sentences, questions can be more adequately considered as 'entities' with non-fixed presuppositions than entities which 'ask' something. The force of asking is derived from this fact: we are 'obliged' to fix presuppositions. And doing this, we only indirectly, so to speak, answer a question. This claim is supported by the meaning of indirect questions: very rarely indirect questions directly 'ask' a question; in most cases, indirect questions indicate a particular epistemic attitude towards a fact expressed by the base of the corresponding direct question and their semantic content precisely allows us to show that questions have non-fixed presuppositions.

A similar reasoning, although maybe more speculative, goes for exclamations and orders. It seems to me that it is possible to show that amazement, surprize, regret, etc. can be indirectly associated with exclamative sentences. According to my proposal, exclamations presuppose their bases. A presupposition is something 'analytically' known and its truth is generally admitted since at some level of the discourse it cannot be negated. Consequently, it describes a necessary event, relative to the universe of discourse. The only 'reasonable' attitude towards an event which is necessary and which cannot be changed is the attitude of amazement, of surprize, of regret, etc. But these are typical emotive attitudes associated with the utterance of an exclamative sentence.

Concerning imperative sentences and the orders they express, we can argue along the following lines. An imperative sentence presupposes the falsity of its base. At some level of the discourse, false presuppositions are not acceptable and they must be 'changed' in one way or another. In some cases where the discourse is very short, i.e. where it takes the form of one imperative sentence, we can change the presupposition or roughly its truth-value,[10] simply by obeying the order expressed by the imperative sentence. The obligation created by the utterance of the imperative sentence is in fact the obligation to 'change' the world in order to make the presupposition true. And this can be done by obeying the order.

5. QUESTIONS AND CONDITIONALS

The present chapter will be more speculative and less precise than the preceding ones. It treats well-established and rather well-known linguistic facts and phenomena whose unified description and explanation have, however, not yet been attempted, as far as I know.

All the semantic intensional relations discussed up to now have one thing in common: the second member of the relation is always a declarative sentence, whereas the first member is either a declarative or a non-declarative sentence. In particular, the relations of presupposition and declaration are relations between sentences of any type and declarative sentences. In the present chapter, I will try to present a relation whose second member is, roughly speaking, a question and whose first member an indicative conditional sentence.

I will try to justify the following claim: a simple indicative conditional sentence 'presupposes' a *yes-no* question whose base is the antecedent of the conditional. Thus, according to the claim I want to defend, the conditional sentence (1) 'presupposes' the question (2).

(1)   If it is raining, Sue will call.
(2)   Is it raining or not?

Of course, I will further specify what I mean by presupposing a question. At this moment, I can already say the following: the description of conditional sentences that I will propose 'contains' in one part, which is devoted to the presupposed content of conditionals, the description of questions that was proposed in chapter 3.

I will be primarily concerned with the description of the so-called *indicative conditionals*, that is, conditionals expressed in the indicative mood. The antecedents of such conditionals can have verbs in the simple past tense, as in (3), or in the present tense, as in (4) and (5):

(3)   If Bill called this morning, he will not come this evening.
(4)   If it is raining now, Bill is in the library.
(5)   If he writes his article this afternoon, you cannot disturb him.

There are other types of conditionals, the so-called *counterfactual* conditionals, which, grammatically, are expressed in the subjunctive mood. Examples of counterfactual conditionals are given in (6) and (7):

(6)   If Bill had been born in Albania, he probably would have spoken Albanian.

(7)   If Mary had called this morning, she would not have been in trouble.

In addition to these grammatical differences, counterfactual conditionals have quite different logical and semantic properties from indicative conditionals. As noted by Stalnaker (1969), only indicative conditionals satisfy the law of transitivity. Thus an inference like the one in (8) is valid:

(8)   If it is raining now, Bill is in the library.
        If Bill is in the library, Sue is not worried.
        Therefore, if it is raining now, Sue is not worried.

According to Stalnaker (1969) and also McCawley (1981: 311), counterfactual conditionals are not transitive, but I must say that I am unable to confirm, or to disconfirm, their intuitions.

McCawley (1981: 312) mentions another semantic difference between the two kinds of conditionals: only indicative conditionals are supposed to allow the addition of material to the antecedent. I must say, however, that neither his example nor many others are clear enough for me to fully grasp his claim. Mc Cawley's example runs as follows:

(9)   If Betty was at the party, Bill enjoyed the party.
        Therefore, if Betty was at the party and they served guacamole, Bill enjoyed the party.

It seems to me that the conclusion is not necessarily valid since it is possible than the displeasure Bill gets being obliged to eat guacamole is much greater that the pleasure he gets from meeting Betty.

I mentioned this difficulty since I believe that we should not rashly apply operations from propositional logic to characterize natural language connectives. Another example of such a misapplication is the attempt to make contrapositions from any, counterfactual or indicative, conditional. It happens very often that contrapositions are simply agrammatical. Consequently, another method for the analysis of conditional sentences must be used. In particular, I will suggest that the notion of 'privative opposition' can be very useful in this case.

With respect to counterfactual conditionals, I will assume, as many others have done before me, that they presuppose the negation of their antecedent. Thus (10) presupposes (11) but does not presuppose (12):

(10)   If Sue had been alone, Bill would have wanted to meet her.

(11)   Sue was not alone.

(12)   Bill did not want to meet her.

This claim follows from our definition of presupposition. Indeed, the opaque sentences (13) and (14) both imply (11):

(13)   Richard regrets that if Sue had been alone Bill would have wanted to meet her.

(14)   Sam does not believe that if Sue had been alone Bill would have wanted to meet her.

Among counterfactual conditionals, one can distinguish 'past' counterfactuals and present counterfactuals. The ones I have discussed up to now are past counterfactuals. The present ones are given in the following examples:

(15)   If I were not at home, you would not be able to speak to me.

(16)   If it were not raining, I would not be wet.

These counterfactuals also presuppose the negation of their antecedent. For instance, (16) presupposes (17) and does not presuppose (18):

(17)   It is raining.

(18)   I am wet.

Theoretically, it is also possible to imagine 'future' counterfactuals: they would presuppose sentences which would be expressed in the future tense and which would correspond to their antecedent sentences. I will not make use of the possibility of such 'future' counterfactuals.

We can now pass on to the discussion of various resemblances between 'standard' indicative conditional sentences and *yes-no* questions. The first type of resemblances that I will take a brief look at are morphological in nature. It is well-known, but still striking, that in many languages the morpheme corresponding to the conjunction used to form an indicative, and less often a counterfactual conditional sentence, is the same as the morpheme which marks direct or indirect questions. Thus, in English, *if* is usually used to form conditional sentences and it is also often used to form indirect questions. In fact, Bolinger (1978) argues that it is only *if* and not *whether* which introduces indirect questions. Similarly, the French morpheme *si* corresponds to the conditional connective and at the same time it can be used as the complementizer introducing questions in indirect interrogative sentences. In other languages, the morpheme which is used to mark a *yes-no* question is formally a part of the conditional connective. Thus, in Russian, the particle *li* which marks a *yes-no* question can also be found in *jes-li*, the marker of the conditional sentence.[11]

The second series of analogies concerns two particular problems in the syntax of interrogatives and conditionals: the behavior of negative polarity items and the word order in these two constructions. As we have seen many times, some expressions do not occur in all possible sentence forms: these are called polarity items. Negative polarity items are not possible in positive sentences:

(19)   *Bill ever imagined this solution.

(20)   *You see anybody.

Interestingly enough, questions and conditionals are contexts which are compatible with negative polarity items:

(21)(a) If Bill ever imagined this solution, his wife would have told me.
    (b) Did Bill ever imagine this solution?

(22)(a) If you see anybody you are drunk.
    (b) Do you see anybody?

A second syntactic similarity is auxiliary inversion (cf. Bolinger 1978). Thus, if one deletes an *if* from an indirect question, one should inverse the auxiliary:

(23)(a) Sue asked if I would call her.
    (b) Sue asked would I call her.

The same phenomena formerly happened in old English to all conditionals, and may still happen to counterfactual conditionals, as Bolinger's examples show:

(24)(a) If I had known you would be offended, I'd have kept quiet.
    (b) Had I known you would be offended, I'd have kept quiet.

(25)(a) If they should agree, send us word.
    (b) Should they agree, send us word.

Furthermore, Bolinger notices an interesting 'discourse' similarity between questions and conditionals. In dramatic speech, question-answer sequences can be used as conditionals by splitting the antecedent and consequent clauses into questions and answers. Bolinger's example goes as follows:

(26)   Did they pay him? He went right to the tavern and spent his wages down to the last dime. Did his wife complain? He beat her. Were the children without food? He never missed his ration.

This discourse similarity has to be connected with pragmatic similarities which I am going to discuss now.

From a pragmatic point of view, one asks a question in order to get some particular information: (27) is normally asked when one does not know whether is was raining yesterday and one wants to know it. But this situation corresponds more or less to the one in which the conditional sentence (28) is uttered: the condition expressed by the antecedent of (28) indicates that the speaker does not know whether it was raining and he wants to know whether it was or not, since only then will he be able to assert what is expressed by the consequent clause of (28):

(27)   Was it raining yesterday?

(28)   If it was raining yesterday, Bill stayed at home.

The fact that such pragmatic conditions are not really necessary for the utterance of a conditional sentence is not essential since, on the one hand, questions can also be uttered in many other situations and, on the other hand, the situation described is a typical situation in which (27) and (28) are produced.

There is another pragmatic aspect connected with the antecedent of a conditional and with a *yes-no* question based on it. Consider (29):

(29)   If she does not arrive tomorrow

This expression is incomplete in quite the same way as the corresponding *yes-no* question (30) is:

(30)   Does she arrive tomorrow?

Both sentences, (29) and (30), should be completed, the first one by the consequent clause and the second one by the answer.

Notice that from a syntactic point of view, antecedents of conditional sentences can be considered as well-formed. In addition, such 'isolated' antecedents may get a 'rhetorical' reading expressing hope, fear, etc. This is clearer in French where antecedents of conditionals can collocate, as such, with the conditional morpheme *si* to express an invitation or a wish; they then play the role of so-called *optatives*. An example is given in (31):

(31)   *Si on allait jouer au shogi.*
        What about a game of *shogi.*

Moreover, in French, some complex sentences containing a counterpart of the English *wh*-question clearly have a 'rhetorical' or 'generic' meaning, usually rendered by a conditional sentence; (32) is paraphrased by (33):

(32)   *Qui parle beaucoup n'est pas triste.*
        The one who talks a lot is not sad.

(33)   *Si quelqu'un parle beaucoup, alors il n'est pas triste.*
          If someone talks a lot he is not sad.

Still, in French, there are complex sentences which are ambiguous between a conditional reading and an indirect interrogative reading; (34) can be translated either by (35a) or by (35b):

(34)   *Tu m'écriras si tu peux venir.*

(35)(a)   You will write me whether you can come or not.
    (b)   If you can come you will write me.

In fact, many indirect interrogatives can be decomposed with the help of conditional sentences, where the base of the embedded question is used as the antecedent of the conditionals. Thus (36a) and (37a) can be paraphrased respectively by (36b) and (37b).

(36)(a)   Bill knows whether Sue is quilty or not.
    (b)   If Sue is guilty, Bill knows that she is guilty and if Sue is not guilty, Bill knows that she is not guilty.

(37)(a)   Everybody can predict whether this problem is decidable.
    (b)   If this problem is decidable, then everybody can predict that it is decidable and if this problem is not decidable, then everybody can predict that it is not decidable.

The results of chapter 3 on questions allow us to make a similar decomposition for direct questions. According to our knowledge of *yes-no* questions, the conditional sentence (39) should be considered as a 'paraphrase' of the question (38):

(38)   Is it true that *P*?
(39)   If *P* then it is presupposed that *P*, and if *not-P* then it is presupposed that *not-P*.

Of course, in order to really understand what (39) says we must first understand what the expression *It is presupposed that P* means. Independently of this problem, (39) indicates, once more, that there is a close relationship between an indicative conditional sentence and a *yes-no* question based on the antecedent of the conditional.

In order to specify the desired relationship between questions and conditionals, let us accept the following definition:

D5.1:   The sentence *It is presupposed that P* is true iff there exists a sentence which presupposes *P*.

In other words, the expression *It is presupposed that P* means that there exists a sentence which presupposes *P*. In particular, the expression *It is presupposed that P or it is presupposed that Q* means that there exists a sentence which presupposes that *P* or which presupposes that *Q*.

According to definition D5.1 and according to the analysis of *yes-no* questions adopted here, the two following expressions should be considered as equivalent:

(40)   The question *Q(S)* exists.

(41)   It is maximally presupposed that *S* or it is maximally presupposed that *not-S*.

Now, the relationship between a conditional sentence and a *yes-no* question based on the antecedent of the conditional can be expressed in the following way: the conditional (42) presupposes (43):

(42)   If *S* then *T*.

(43)   There exists the *yes-no* question *Q(S)*.

This means that (44), for instance, presupposes the existence of the question (45):

(44)   If Bill solved the problem, he (=Bill) is free.

(45)   Did Bill solve the problem?

To justify this claim, we have to show that a conditional sentence such as (42) maximally presupposes *S* or maximally presupposes *not-S*.

Consider once again (44). This sentence can be paraphrased, it seems to me, by the following complex sentence:

(46)   [Bill is free because he solved the problem] or [If Bill had solved the problem he would have been free].

Indeed, the antecedent of (44) is either true or false. When it is true, then the first disjunct of (46), given in (47), is true. When the antecedent of (44) is false, then, given the relation indicated by the whole conditional, the second disjunct, represented by the counterfactual (48), is true:

(47)   Bill is free because he solved the problem.

(48)   If Bill had solved the problem, he would have been free.

Notice in addition that both disjuncts, (47) and (48), express in some way the fact that (44) is a conditional sentence: in (47) by the presence of the causal disjunction *because*, and in (48) by the counterfactual conditional. Causal sentences bear some kind of inverse relation to conditionals, and counterfactual conditionals probably contain the same assertion as the corresponding indicative conditional but they have some special presuppositions. These rather special relations between indicative conditionals on the one hand and causal sentences and counterfactual conditionals on the other hand can be better described by means of the notion of privative opposition. I think that the following claim can be justified: indicative conditionals are in privative opposition to counterfactuals and to some causative sentences. More precisely, this means, according to the definition of privative opposition given in the first chapter, that (48) for instance intensionally asserts (44) and that (48) has a particular presupposition absent from (44). As I have already mentioned, one such presupposition is precisely the negation of the antecedent of (48). Similarly, the causal sentence (47) intensionally asserts (44) and presupposes a sentence absent from the set of presuppositions of (44). This presupposition is precisely the antecedent of the indicative conditional (44).

In conclusion, we have the following situation: (47) presupposes (49) and (48) presupposes (50):

(49)   Bill solved the problem.
(50)   Bill did not solve the problem.

These presuppositions can be considered as presuppositions proper to the marked terms of a privative opposition. We can show this also in a more direct way by using our definition of presupposition or rather some of its consequences. Thus we notice that opaque sentences in which (47) is embedded imply (49). For instance, both (51) and (52) imply (49):

(51)   Sam thinks that Bill is free because he solved the problem.
(52)   Sue regrets that Bill is free because he solved the problem.

So far, we have obtained the following result: the first conjunct of (46) presupposes the antecedent of the conditional sentence (44) and the second conjunct of (46) presupposes the negation of the antecedent of (44). So, at present, I have shown that (44) implies (46) which presupposes either the antecedent of (44) or the negation of the antecedent. More generally, using methods similar to those used above, the following can be established: the past indicative conditional (53) implies the expression (54) which implies the existence of the question (55) based on the antecedent of (53):

(53)   If S past cond. T.
(54)   [T because S] or [S past counterfactual cond. T].
(55) $Q(S)$.

This does not correspond to what we were looking for since we want to establish that the existence of (55) is presupposed. But this can still be done if we take into account that the negation of (53) also implies an expression which implies the existence of (55). Indeed, the negation of (53) is equivalent to something like (56):

(56)   [T not because S] or [S past counterfactual cond. *not-T*].

For the concrete example (44), its normal negation (57) implies (58):

(57)   If Bill solved the problem he is not free.
(58)   [It is not because Bill solved the problem that he is free] or [If Bill had solved the problem he would not have been free].

Now, the first conjunct of (58) presupposes the antecedent of (57) and the second conjunct of (58) presupposes the negation of the antecedent. Consequently, if the above implication between (57) and (58) is true, the negation of the conditional (44) also implies the existence of an expression implying the existence of the question based on the antecedent of the conditional. So, since a conditional and its negation imply the existence of the question based on the antecedent of the conditional, and according to the consequence of the definition of presupposition stating that for declarative sentences the classical definition holds, we can say that the desired result is established, at least for past indicative conditionals.[12]

The reasoning for present tense indicative conditionals is quite similar: instead of using the past counterfactual in the interpretational sentence, we use the present counterfactual. The situation is a bit more complicated for a special type of indicative conditionals, namely future indicative conditionals, which exist formally in some languages. In Polish, for instance, parallel to a present indicative conditional like (59), one can also find future conditionals, which formally correspond to a questionable form like (60):

(59)   If Bill writes his thesis, he is free.
(60)   ?If Bill will write his thesis he will be free.

To illustrate the difficulty with such future conditionals, let us use an example of a *semantically* future conditional. Consider (61):

(61)   If you call me tomorrow, I will answer this question.

If we want to analyze this conditional in the way the preceding one was analyzed, we should consider that it is equivalent to a disjunction the first disjunct of which is given in (62):

(62)   I will answer this question (tomorrow) because you will call me
        tomorrow.

The second disjunct should be parallel to (48) but should relate to the future.
In other words, the second disjunct should be expressed by a 'future counterfactual', which would presuppose the negation of its antecedent sentence.
The notion of a 'future' counterfactual is in some sense internally contradictory
and we know that neither English nor many other languages have such a future
conditional form. Of course, this does not mean that my proposal is invalid,
but only that the methods used to justify it are not applicable to all cases.

Before making some general remarks about presupposing the existence of
a question, the method applied here, and the possibility of an analysis of conditionals, I would like to say a few words about other constructions which may
presuppose the existence of questions. Good candidates for such constructions
are, it seems to me, all constructions which 'indirectly imply' questions or which
give rise to a *derived* interrogative illocutionary force. Among them is a class
which we have already partially analyzed, the class of indirect questions.

There are two ways to show that indirect questions presuppose the existence
of questions expressed by their embedded complements. First, we can break
indirect questions up into a disjunction of two disjuncts such that one disjunct
presupposes the base of the question and the other one presupposes the negation
of the base. The second way, related to the first one, considers that indirect
questions imply the base or their negation, and since they are opaque sentences,
they, roughly, presuppose what they can imply.

It is not difficult to tell the difference between an indirect question and an
indicative conditional sentence whose antecedent is the base of the question:
since both of them are declarative sentences, they have different assertions and
declarations. Thus (63) and (64) clearly imply quite different things:

(63)   Bill knows whether it is raining or not.
(64)   If it is raining, Sue will come alone.

But this is not the only difference: both sentences also have different presuppositions. Thus (63) presupposes (65) and (64) presupposes (66):

(65)   There exist someone whose name is *Bill*.
(66)   Sue will come.

In other words, neither conditional sentences nor indirect questions presuppose
maximally what the corresponding direct interrogatives presuppose. The particular presuppositions in question, (65) and (66), are neither entailed by the base

of the indirect question, nor by the antecedent of the conditional or their negation.

The difference between maximal and non-maximal presuppositions is essential in order to understand the difference between direct and indirect questions. One would be tempted to say that the difference between a direct question such as

(67)   Is it raining?

and an indirect question such as (63) is the following: the direct question asserts its own existence, and the indirect question (with the same base) and the conditional sentence whose antecedent constitutes the base presuppose the existence of the direct question. But this claim is not very clear since we do not know what it means for a question to assert its own existence. Furthermore, we know that a *yes-no* question disjunctively presupposes its base, as does the corresponding indirect question. So, in fact, direct as well as indirect questions presuppose the existence of the corresponding question since both disjunctively presuppose the base. So how to describe the difference? We know that there are many possibilities: indirect questions are declaratives and as such they declare something whereas direct questions, being non-declarative sentences, do not declare anything. I have suggested, but did not show, that this difference is a corollary of the difference in the maximality of presuppositions: both types of interrogative sentences disjunctively presuppose their base but only direct interrogatives presuppose it maximally; indirect questions have some presuppositions which are not entailed by the base of the embedded question.

The condition of maximality of presuppositions was introduced for the following reason: it permits us to reject as interrogatives those expressions which, although they trivially presuppose a possible base, clearly are not either direct or indirect questions. Consider (68):

(68)   Bill knows that it is raining.

Since this sentence presupposes its complement sentence, it is trivially true that it presupposes it disjunctively. In other words, the following statement is trivially true:

(69)   Sentence (68) presupposes its complement, or it presupposes the negation of its complement.

So, if it were not for the condition of maximality of the disjunctive presupposition, (68) would have to be considered as a *yes-no* question based on its complement. But we know that the presupposition indicated in (69) is not a maximal one – (68) also presupposes (65) – and consequently, (68) is not a direct question.

Why, however, can we not consider (68) as an indirect question? I have defined an indirect question as an opaque sentence which syntactically contains a 'direct' question and which, semantically, carries an interrogative force. Furthermore, I have suggested that the interrogative force may be due to the disjunctive presupposition, i.e. to the fact that one possible presupposition must be fixed. But (68) only artificially has a disjunctive presupposition – it only presupposes its complement sentence and never the negation of the complement sentence. And this fact is 'analytically' known: only the form of the complementizer and the lexical value of the composing items are sufficient. On the other hand, in the case of (63), where we have a 'real' indirect question, we cannot 'analytically' know which sentence is presupposed; all we can 'analytically' determine is that either the complement sentence or its negation are presupposed: we cannot say which one just by looking at the linguistic material. To find out which sentence is presupposed, we must know what the world is like. This difference between factive sentences like (68) and indirect questions like (63) is indicated by the form of the complementizer.

The linguistic form and the semantic content of the opaque operator are also determinative in the case of other types of non-declaratives. Thus only (70) and not (71) should be considered as an indirect exclamative sentence:

(70)   Sue knows what a fool Bill is.
(71)   Sue knows that Bill is a fool.

Although (70) and (71) have exactly the same set of presuppositions, they do not express the same content, neither directly nor indirectly, because formally, their complement sentences are not identical: only (70) is marked as containing an exclamative complement. To my mind, this is in agreement with Grimshaw's (1979) claim that complement taking verbs select a particular semantic type or a particular non-declarative sentence.

I have made this somewhat lengthy expansion on direct, indirect, and 'almost' indirect non-declaratives in order to point out various difficulties that the initial idea of an indicative conditional presupposing the existence of a question can meet with, however attractive it may be at the beginning. The mechanism of indirectly inducing illocutionary forces is far from clear for all cases. The claim I have tried to justify concerns only the necessary conditions which such a mechanism should account for. The discussion of factive sentences which can presuppose the base (or its negation) of possible non-declaratives shows that the sufficient conditions cannot be easily expressed.

There is also a terminological difficulty with my proposal. To specify the claim, I used the following abbreviation:

(72)   *It is presupposed that S* means that there exists a sentence which presupposes *S*.

But what is it to say that a sentence *S*, or more generally that a sign *S*, exists? If we think in terms of *sign types*, given the usual way of introducing the lexicon and the syntax, (72) is trivially true for any sentence *S* since there exist types of every sentence and, in particular, of those which presuppose *S*. In other words, if we think about sign types, then everything is presupposed. To avoid this clearly undesirable consequence, we can regard signs as tokens. This way of analyzing at least some linguistic signs would give us a way of talking of utterances and not of sentences. And we know that, in the case of derived meanings, it is more adequate to consider utterances, given the importance of the contexts, instead of considering sentence types or sentences independently of the context. But, clearly, this move would lead to various technical difficulties. We do not really know how to treat sentence tokens, when to oppose them to sentence types, how to interpret them semantically, etc.

In spite of these difficulties, I would like to continue my speculations, turning back to some suggestions made above concerning the semantic relations between conditional sentences and their representations. Briefly, I will try to say something about the semantic status of conditional sentences as such.

Indicative as well as subjunctive conditional 'connectives' are known to play a very special role among the classical 'logical' connectives. The point which is of interest for us here is that conditional connectives behave very specially with respect to non-declarative sentences. Thus, in opposition to the conjunction *and* and the disjunction *or*, no non-declarative sentence can be connected with another sentence by means of *if . . . then*. Thus we have (73) and (74) but (75), (76), and (77) are impossible:

(73)   Who called and what did Sue write?

(74)   Is it raining or is it snowing?

(75)   *Who called then I will come.

(76)   *How beautiful she is then I will look at her.

(78)   *Let Bill close the door then I will speak.

On the other hand, non-declarative sentences can take the place of the consequent clause:

(78)   If it rains, take your umbrella.

(79)   If Sue did not call, then who called.

As far as I can judge, exclamative sentences cannot assume the position of consequent clauses in conditional sentences.

Of course, disjunction and conjunction cannot freely connect sentences of different types. In addition, there seems to be an asymmetry in what type of sentences can precede and follow another type. Thus, in general, declaratives cannot follow non-declaratives in conjunctions and disjunctions, except when a declarative sentence follows an imperative sentence:

(80)   Give her a call and she will come.

(81)   Close the door or she will get cold.

(82)(a) Joe will buy it and who will drink it?

  (b)*Who will drink it and Joe will buy it.

(83)   *Close the door or who will do it?

(84)   *Is it raining or close the door.

All these examples show that it is not easy to understand what is going on and that we are far from applying the simple formation rules of connectives to declarative sentences. Moreover, in the case of conditional connectives, important semantic changes can occur in the connected sentences. In particular, orders and questions can be subject to special conditions. Thus we have conditional questions as in (85) and conditional orders as in (86):

(85)(a) If it is going to rain, are you taking an umbrella?

  (b) If it were to rain, would you take an umbrella?

(86)   If you go out, buy me the New York Times!

In fact, it is usually emphasized that there is a big difference between sentences like (85a), called (proper) *conditional questions*, and sentences like (85b), called *hypothetical questions* (cf. Belnap and Steel 1976: 95). The latter, but not the former, can be conceived as arising from a logical operation on an assertion (the condition expressed by the antecedent clause) and a question (or an answer to the question). Thus the direct answers to (85b) should contain *if*:

(87)(a) Yes, if it were to rain, I would take an umbrella.

  (b) No, if it were to rain, I would not take an umbrella.

On the other hand, conditional questions like (85a) do not call for answers having the form of a conditional sentence, but rather 'ask' that an answer, which can be unconditional in form, be supplied, only if a certain condition, the one expressed by the antecedent, is fulfilled. Thus, theoretically, (85a) can be answered either by (88a) or by (88b):

(88)(a) Yes, I am taking an umbrella.

(b) No, I am not taking an umbrella.

Similarly, (86) expresses an order to be accomplished and obeyed only if a certain condition, in this case the one expressed by the antecedent clause, is true.

In any case, conditional orders and conditional questions differ from 'ordinary' orders and questions in that their illocutionary force can be suspended, and in that they depend on the satisfaction of a particular condition, explicitly mentioned in the antecedent clause. This is only a particular case of presupposition suspension in the context of conditional sentences, and consequently, the description of conditional sentences should account for the above restrictions, irrespective of the type of constituent sentences, in terms of the relations between presupposed and asserted content.

The first presuppositional property of conditional sentences has already been established, *viz*. when we were dealing with the relation between conditionals and *yes-no* questions: an indicative conditional sentence disjunctively presupposes its antecedent, i.e., the conditional sentence either presupposes its antecedent ot it presupposes the negation of its antecedent. The other properties of conditional sentences can be obtained from their decomposition into the disjunction of a counterfactual sentence and a causative sentence. Concerning counterfactual conditionals, I suggested considering that they presuppose the negations of their antecedent sentences.

The situation is more complicated with causative sentences. Thus (89) is clearly composed of (90) and (91):

(89)   Bill is free because he solved the problem.

(90)   Bill is free.

(91)   Bill solved the problem.

The problem is now to determine whether (89) presupposes (90) and (91), or whether it presupposes just one sentence and asserts the other one. We have already assumed that (91) is presupposed by (89). It is not easy to give strong arguments for this claim because it is not quite clear what type of causation we are dealing with in cases like (89). For the same reason, it is not easy to decide what the status of (90) is. This difficulty may be solved if we consider indicative conditionals as the unmarked counterpart of counterfactual conditionals and of special causative sentences. Formally, counterfactuals look very much

102 NON-DECLARATIVE SENTENCES

like indicative conditionals; in addition, they have special morphological marks which often characterize the marked terms of a privative opposition. Moreover, the semantic requirement also seems to be met: counterfactual conditionals imply their corresponding indicative conditionals. Thus (92) is implied by (93), the supposed marked term of the opposition:

(92)   If Bill solved the problem, he is free.

(93)   If Bill had solved the problem, he would have been free.

According to the definition of privative opposition, a sentence privatively op-posed to another one is its proper intensional assertion. This means, according to the definition of intensional assertion, that the negation of the marked sen-tence should imply the negation of the corresponding unmarked one. In our case, this means that the presupposition preserving negation of (93) should imply the presupposition preserving negation of (92). The corresponding ne-gations of (93) and (92) are given in (94) and (95) respectively:

(94)   If Bill had solved the problem, he would not have been free.

(95)   If Bill solved the problem, he is not free.

Indeed, since (93) as a counterfactual conditional presupposes the negation of its antecedent, the negation of (93) also should presuppose the negation of the antecedent of (93). Indeed, (94) also presupposes the negation of the ante-cedent of (93). Furthermore, if (93) implies (92), then (94) implies (95) since both (93) and (94) have the same 'sentence form'. And given our understanding of conditionals, it seems to me that we can claim that (93) implies (92).

Now, we know that a given sentence can be privatively opposed to two sentences. For instance, *to know whether* is privatively opposed to *to know that* and to *to know that not* and these two 'marked' terms have presupposi-tions that take opposite truth-values. I have proposed that indicative condi-tional sentences can also be privatively opposed to special 'causative' sentences. To know what properties such causative sentences have, we should compare them with the other marked terms, the counterfactual conditionals: we know that, in particular, they must have mutually contradictory presuppositions. This condition is satisfied if we consider the causative sentence (96) as another marked counterpart in its opposition to (92) and that (96) presupposes (97):

(96)   Bill is free because he solved the problem.

(97)   Bill solved the problem.

Indeed, the truth value of (97) is opposite to that of the presupposition of the counterfactual conditional, which I consider as another marked counterpart of the indicative conditional (92).

Now, since (96) is a marked counterpart of (92), its normal negation – or, rather, something corresponding to the normal negation – should imply the negation of (92), which is implied by the negation of the first marked counterpart; in addition, this negation should also presuppose (97). It seems to me that (98) is the negation we are looking for:[13]

(98)   Bill is not free because he solved the problem.
        (Although Bill solved the problem he is not free.)

Notice in addition that what is negated in both marked counterparts can be roughly considered as corresponding to the assertion of the indicative conditional sentence, or at least to one disjunct of the assertion. This asserted part corresponds roughly to the consequent clause of the conditional.

From the above considerations, the following interpretation of indicative conditional sentences emerges: (99) is further explicitated by the disjunction in (100):

(99)   If S then T.
(100)   The conditional (99) presupposes S and asserts T or it presupposes *not-S* and *not-T*.

In particular, it follows from this description that if the antecedent of the conditional is false, then the consequent is false, but its falsity is then presupposed and not stated directly. This fact captures, it seems to me, the old idea that indicative conditionals, as opposed to the material implication, in some sense imply their converse: the sentence *If S then T* carries the information that *If not-S then not-T*. This information can be suspended, or negated, in the same way as presuppositions can be suspended or negated.

The essential property of the above description, which distinguishes it from most other descriptions of conditional sentences, is that it contains a disjunction of presuppositions and, in some sense, a disjunction of assertions. Although the exact status of a disjunctive implication is not quite clear for me, it seems that a description containing a disjunction of properties roughly indicates that these properties are not decidable by the form alone of the constituents, but depend on the properties of the (non-linguistic) world. Depending on what the world is like, either one or the other disjunct is true. Thus conditionals, just like questions, are 'semantically undecidable' since their semantic properties depend on the external world.

6. TENTATIVE CONCLUSIONS

Many things we know about natural languages, in particular about their learnability and about their structural analysis, force us to recognize the existence of linguistic rules. Different aspects of language may require different types of rules. Syntactic aspects of languages require syntactic rules and semantic aspects semantic rules. The rules are needed because, without them, some forms cannot be recognized and their meaning cannot be captured. Linguistic rules are in principle recursive, which means that they supply an algorithm by means of which we can work out any essential property or linguistic aspect concerning the meaning or the structure of a portion of natural language. The semantic rules are used to 'calculate' various aspects of the meaning of accepted and recognized linguistic structures. In particular, the job of semantic rules is to describe and to predict semantic relations of an implicative type, and especially intensional relations like those introduced in the first chapter.

In this last, concluding chapter I would like to take up again the main ideas of this discussion and the main results to which they have led, and incorporate them into a description of a formal language which may more clearly serve as a model describing the phenomena we are dealing with. In particular, some characteristics of the formal language, especially its semantic rules, may be useful for a better understanding of the main ideas that I used in my approach of non-declarative sentences.

Suppose that we have a language L with specific syntactic rules. These rules provide us in particular with the notion of 'basic sentences' in L. Basic sentences correspond to declarative sentences in natural languages. The sentence category is evidently not the only category in L: many other primitive categories are introduced by special lexical rules, and an unlimited number of derived categories is given by some schema of rules. These rules, introducing the syntactic categories of L, are the rules used in one version or other of a categorial grammar.

The purpose of another group of rules is to transform the structure of complex expressions to which these rules apply. In so doing, they may, but need not, change the category of the input expressions. As such, a rule may change the elements of the sentence category into the category of nouns; this type of rules transforms (1) into (2) for instance:

(1)   The girl ate an artichoke.

(2)   The girl who ate an artichoke.

These transformational rules are purely syntactic rules; they operate only on the syntactic structure and they do not introduce any 'new' lexical items. This means that they should be distinguished from the purely formative rules which govern the application of functional elements to their possible arguments. Such lexical transformation rules transform for instance singular noun phrases into plural ones. Similarly, they may transform a basic sentence into its negation or into its future tense counterpart; (1) may be transformed into (3) or (4):

(3)   The girl did not eat an artichoke.

(4)   The girl will eat an artichoke.

At present, it is less important to know whether negation or future tense operate on the level of sentences or verb phrases. What is essential is the fact that, in this case, we are not dealing with purely syntactic transformations: the negation introduces a 'new' lexical item which applies to the sentence (to the verb phrase) to yield a new sentence (verb phrase). Similarly, the future tense transformation is the application of a function expression of the category VP/VP to an expression of the category VP.

Now, the language L contains purely syntactic transformations. In particular, some syntactic transformations in L operate on basic sentences and yield non-basic sentences as output. This means roughly that some purely syntactic rules transform declarative sentences into non-declarative ones. On the other hand, it seems to me that it is an open empirical question whether the language L, supposed to model natural languages, should have purely syntactic transformations whose input and output is the set of basic sentences. Should there be basic sentences related by a purely syntactic transformation, then these sentences very likely are not semantically equivalent: they do not have the same set of semantic consequences. Thus the 'active' sentence (1) and its passive counterpart (5) do not seem to be related by a purely syntactic transformation:

(5) An artichoke was eaten by the girl.

Indeed, very likely, the passive results from the application of the 'passive' operator to the 'active' verb phrase. On the other hand, some sentences which are very likely related by a purely syntactic transformation are not semantically equivalent. This is in particular the case with privatively opposed sentences.

We will assume that, if a purely syntactic transformation applies to a given sentence, then the resulting sentence is syntactically more complex than the input sentence. Such a non-basic sentence, obtained by applying purely syntactic transformations to a basic sentence, corresponds to a non-declarative sentence in natural language. This means that the number of purely syntactic transformations must be limited and that a special subset of 'non-declarative' purely syntactic transformations must be distinguished. These are applicable only once to basic sentences in order to produce non-basic sentences. If we accept a kind of 'illocutionary' ambiguity in that some non-declarative sentences are ambiguous with respect to their type, then some non-declarative transformations may apply to non-basic sentences: in this case, one can obtain a non-declarative sentence from another non-declarative sentence.

As I have said, apart from sentences, the language L contains many syntactic 'primitive' types. Since we want to treat presuppositions and non-declarative sentences in L, it must contain unary sentential operators and, in particular, unary normally opaque operators. Whether the opacity is a syntactic or semantic phenomenon is not quite clear to me. Since we want the formation rules of structures with opaque operators to be recursive, we must mark in the lexicon which operators are opaque and which are not. This move may appear somewhat arbitrary since in natural language the opacity of many operators is rather a semantic feature: this is because opaque operators are usually syntactically complex.[14] They are composed of a subject NP and of a kind of transitive verb. Now, depending on the referent of the subject NP, some sentential operators may or may not be opaque. As such, the operator *He knows that* is probably not opaque if the pronoun *he* refers to God, who is supposed to be omniscient. Another difficulty with opaque operators is that they usually have a so-called transparent reading and that, on this reading, the substitution of many co-extensional arguments is possible.

These difficulties should not force us, however, to give up the syntactic specification of opaque operators. In particular, this classification can be made by means of presuppositions: some special syntactic features will be associated with some particular presuppositions. For instance, all sentential operators specified as opaque can be considered as roughly presupposing the non-omniscience of the referent of the corresponding subject NP.

This technique of associating presuppositions with a specific syntactic feature becomes clearer when we treat binary connectives, which of course the language L must contain. Natural language connectives are subject to various semantic constraints. Consider the following sentences:

(6)   *Bill called and Bill called.
(7)   Bill called and Joe called.
(8)   Bill sold the car to Joe and Joe bought the car from Bill.

Sentence (6) should probably be considered as syntactically ill-formed. Its ill-formedness is a consequence of the formation rule saying something to the effect that a binary connective cannot connect two identical sentences. Now, this formation rule cannot exclude sentence (8) which is also very strange, but rather for semantic reasons. Sentence (8) has a false presupposition because (8) is a conjunction of two different sentences expressing the same proposition. More generally, the following presupposition should be attached to the formation rule for the conjunction *and*: (9) presupposes (10):

(9)   *S and T.*
(10)   Sentences S and T do not express the same proposition.

This general 'metalinguistic' presupposition forces us to consider (11) as a presupposition of (7):

(11)   Bill and Joe are different persons.

If (11) is false, (7) is of course 'still' well-formed but it then contains a false presupposition, just as (8) is syntactically well-formed although it has a false presupposition.

I have discussed this problem of presuppositions of binary connectives at greater length, since in L, binary connectives connect not only basic (declarative) sentences but also non-basic (non-declarative) sentences. In chapter 5, I have shown that well-formedness conditions for conjunctions or disjunctions of non-declarative sentences are very complicated. The reason is, it seems to me, that it is often very difficult to judge whether the ill-formedness involved is of a semantic or syntactic type. Thus consider (12) and (13):

(12)   Bill called and who wrote a letter?
(13)   ?Who wrote a letter and Bill called.

Sentence (13), as opposed to (12), seems ill-formed. Now, the only difference between (12) and (13) is the difference in the order of the conjoined sentences. It seems to me that we cannot impose, at least not for the conjunction *and*, asymmetry as a syntactic condition on well-formedness. We know that even 'declarative' *and* may seem asymmetrical, as the following examples show:

(14)   Joe called and only Joe called.
(15)   Only Joe called and Joe called.

We know that conjoined sentences have particular presuppositions which may be absent from their conjuncts and that they can vary when the order of the conjuncts varies (cf. Zuber 1979). Since the illocutionary force of non-declarative sentences is presupposed, it is quite possible that the restrictions on the type of arguments binary connectives can take should also be expressed in the form of particular 'metalinguistic' presuppositions.

The last comment that I would like to make about the difficulties of the proper introduction of the 'syntax' of L concerns the necessity of specifying the incompatibility between some purely syntactic transformations and the application of some lexical rules. We know that non-declarative sentences cannot be embedded in non-opaque operators. For the language L, this means that non-basic sentences cannot serve as arguments of non-opaque sentential operators.

Suppose that the syntax of L is specified correctly and, that this specification avoids all the above difficulties. What is then the purpose of the semantics of L? In my opinion, it should account for all the implicative semantic relations I have discussed in the preceding chapters. A very special implicative relation I have often mentioned is the disjunctive implication or disjunctive presupposition. This relation is far from trivial. For instance, it is not true that a disjunction of two sentences disjunctively implies every disjunct. More precisely, (16) is not true:

(16)   The disjunction (S or T) semantically implies S or it semantically implies T.

On the other hand, a conjunction of two sentences trivially implies each of the conjuncts disjunctively; (17) is trivially true:

(17)   The conjunction (S and T) semantically implies S or it semantically implies T.

Similarly, any sentence S disjunctively implies itself and any other declarative sentence T. This means that (18) is trivially true:

(18)   A sentence S semantically implies S or it implies T.

When speaking about disjunctive implication, for instance in the case of questions, I added a supplementary condition of *maximality*: a sentence S maximally implies a sentence T iff S implies T and any sentence implied by S is also implied by T. One can easily verify that a conjunction does not maximally and disjunctively imply each of its conjuncts; (19) is not generally true:

(19)   The conjunction (S and T) maximally implies S or it maximally implies T.

Clearly, any sentence S maximally and disjunctively implies itself and any other sentence T; (20) is trivially true:

(20)   A sentence S maximally implies S or it maximally implies T.

That (20) is trivially true can be grasped better if we replace T by *not-S*:

(21)   A sentence S maximally implies S or it maximally implies *not-S*.

The expression (21) is trivially true because its second disjunct is never true.

Now, we have seen that there are expressions, in particular indirect interrogative sentences, which can (non-trivially) disjunctively imply something different from themselves. For instance, I based my analysis of *yes-no* questions on the fact that an indirect question like (22) disjunctively (but not maximally) implies its complement sentence and its negation. In other words, I considered (23) to be true:

(22)   Bill knows whether P or not.
(23)   Sentence *Bill knows whether P or not-P* implies P or it implies *not-P*.

The truth of (23) is based on the equivalence between (22) and (24) and on the fact that, roughly, *to know that P* implies P:

(24)   Bill knows that P or Bill knows that *not-P*.

The equivalence between (22) and (24) and the fact that factive sentences imply their complement are not sufficient to ensure the truth of (23). Indeed, a disjunction may be true in two different situations ('possible worlds') without one of the disjuncts being true in these situations.

To obtain the truth of (23), I assumed an additional condition: I considered that the properties of the subjects of factive constructions are in some sense 'rigid' properties. More precisely, I assumed that there are no two possible worlds w_i and w_j such that (25) is true in w_i and (26) is true in w_j:

(25)   Bill knows that P.
(26)   Bill knows that *not-P*.

This means, roughly, that the properties an individual acquires when 'changing' with possible worlds cannot have contradictory presuppositions. In other words, in two different worlds, an individual can have contradictory properties (*to know that P* vs. *not to know that P*) but he cannot have contrary properties (*to know that P* vs. *to know that not-P*).

I offered just one argument to support this assumption, which is based on the phenomenon of privative opposition. I said that privative oppositions are linguistic, or semantic, properties of some constructions, or rather of some pairs of constructions. Furthermore, I assumed that such linguistic properties cannot change with possible worlds. Thus we know that (22) can be privatively opposed either to (25) or to (26), and that the choice of the marked term just depends on the situation in the world: if (25) is true then, clearly, (26) cannot be the marked term of the opposition.

There is a small difference between this opposition and the 'classical' opposition illustrated by the two following examples:

(27)   Leslie is a poet.

(28)   Leslie is a poetess.

Here we have to do with a formally marked privative opposition: the marked term of the opposition, represented by sentence (28), is chosen without ambiguity. Notice, however, that this case also involves a disjunctive implication:

(29)   *Leslie is a poet* implies *Leslie is a man* or it implies *Leslie is a woman.*

Of course, (29) is true only if we assume that the presupposed property (of being a man or a woman) is a rigid property, which seems very natural.

I concede that my argument for considering some properties determined by presuppositions as rigid is not a very strong one. The exact status of these properties depends on the semantics of L and on its 'ontology'. However, it is clear that, given the fact that privative oppositions are considered as linguistic universals, the semantics of L should be able to treat the phenomenon of privative oppositions, preferably by means of disjunctive implications. The use of privative oppositions in the domain of non-declarative sentences becomes important if we realize that they can explain the derivation mechanism of various 'indirect' or 'non-literal' readings which some non-declaratives may produce. Thus the questions in (a) can have, with a special intonation, the 'declarative' readings in (b):

(30)(a) Didn't she call yesterday?

(b) She called yesterday.

(31)(a) Who will eat it?

(b) Nobody will eat it.

The derived 'declarative' readings correspond to the negation of one of the presuppositions of the questions. Now, we know that the unmarked term of a privative opposition can have a 'derived' reading roughly equivalent to the negation of the marked term, or when the unmarked term is negated, then its 'derived' reading is equal to the presupposition of the marked term. Thus (32a), with a special intonation, may mean (32b) and (33a) may mean (33b):

(32)(a) Leslie is a *poet* (and not a *poetess*).

(b) Leslie is a man.

(33)(a) Leslie is not a *poet* (Leslie is a *poetess*).

(b) Leslie is a woman.

Thus, in a special situation, with a special intonation, the privatively opposed terms become 'polarly' opposed, which means that their presuppositions are in contradiction. Since this is impossible, at this level, the presuppositions cease to be presuppositions; this is probably due to the fact that a special intonation removes the opacity of the corresponding operators or that negation is not opacity preserving. Thus indirect questions become polarly, and not privatively, opposed to their 'indirect' declaratives. This means that the sentential operator, in the indirect question and the corresponding 'marked' indirect declarative, ceases to be opaque. For instance, (34), with a special intonation, can be interpreted as (35):

(34)   Bill did not know that she did not call yesterday.
(35)   Bill did not know that she did not call yesterday because she called yesterday.

On such an interpretation, where the presupposed complement sentence is false, negation is not opacity preserving. Furthermore, the corresponding indirect question will, semantically speaking, consist of a non-opaque operator:

(36)   Bill did not know whether she called yesterday or not.

Thus, although(36) normally disjunctively implies its complement and the negation of the complement, in this case, it will imply (37) because of the 'special' reading given to (34):

(37)   She called yesterday.

The same reasoning is possible with all indirect questions in which the question (30a) is embedded. In other words, indirect questions will have non-opaque operators, or rather opaque operators with a non-opaque reading.

This property of indirect questions permits us to understand why direct questions can get derived 'declarative' readings. Indeed, we know that 'direct' questions do not declare anything because the only relation into which they enter with their bases is the presupposition relation; this is so because direct questions cannot be embedded in non-opaque operators. I have just shown that, in some special situations, indirect questions 'assert' their base or their negation, because the sentential operator constituting the indirect questions, or the negation of the sentential operator, 'ceases' to be opaque. But this means that, in those situations, the corresponding direct questions declare something: they declare the negation of the presupposition given by the marked term of the privative opposition into which the indirect questions enter. Thus, although 'normally' (direct) questions do not declare anything, in some situations, with a special intonation, they can 'indirectly' declare something: they then declare the sentences expressing the rhetorical readings of questions.

Interestingly enough, imperative and exclamative sentences do not have 'rhetorical' readings; they never declare anything. To my mind, this corresponds to the fact that indirect imperatives and indirect exclamations do not enter into privative oppositions because there is no second member of the opposition. Consequently, indirect imperatives and indirect exclamations are always opaque sentences and as such they never declare anything.

Of course, rhetorical questions are only a special case involving indirect or non-literal readings. Any theory of non-declarative sentences should account for the variety of phenomena in which indirect derivation occurs. Let me mention one special series of them.

The best known case is that of indirect conditional orders which some questions may induce. Thus, as is well-known, (38) can indirectly express (39):

(38)   Can you close the door?
(39)   If you can (close the door), close the door!

According to my analysis of conditional sentences, an analysis which may be done irrespective of the type of the consequent clause, the conditional (39) 'presupposes' the question (38). Furthermore, both the imperative sentence which is the consequent clause of (39) and the question (38) presuppose (40):

(40)   You are not closing the door.

Indeed, if (40) were false, (38) would be in some sense nonsensical.

The following situation arises: the derived reading of the expression A is represented by the expression B, which presupposes A. This seems to be a very common situation of non-literal readings. I have already mentioned the case of *to have* vs *to buy/sell*. For instance, (41) indirectly implies (42):

(41)   Do you have the NYT?
(42)   If you have the NYT, give/sell me the NYT.

But we also know that *to give* or *to sell* presupposes *to have*. Another illustration of this mechanism is the derivation of a conditional question from a direct question. Thus the question (43) in some way indirectly implies the conditional question (44):

(43)   Did someone call?
(44)   If someone called who was it (who called)?

Indeed, (43) is usually answered either by (45a) or by (45b), which strictly speaking are answers to (44):

(45)(a) Yes, Bill.
    (b) No, no one.

Here also, according to my analysis of conditional sentences, (44) presupposes (43), and nothing else.

What is important in these examples is the fact that in all of them the derived reading is based on the question whose indirect counterpart seems to be determined by the marked term. By this I mean that it is impossible to get the derived reading from the question whose second disjunct is explicitly given. Thus (46), (47), and (48) do not carry the indirect readings given by (39), (42), and (44), respectively:

(46)   Can you close the door or not?

(47)   Do you have the NYT or not?

(48)   Did someone call or not?

This suggests that the indirect questions containing the direct ones, which give rise to the derived readings, have already selected their marked counterparts.[15]

Furthermore, in all these cases, the derived reading maximally presupposes the sentence from which it is derived. More precisely, the situation can be described as follows: there is a sentence S, of which we know that it is a presupposition of another sentence.

Notice that, strictly speaking, not only questions give rise to this type of derived readings. Thus the conditional sentence (49) indirectly 'implies' (50):

(49)   If you do not close the window the bird will fly away.

(50)   Close the window! because if you do not close the window the bird will fly away.

In my analysis of conditional sentences, I suggested that they are privatively opposed either to counterfactual conditionals or to special causative sentences. Furthermore, I also suggested that causative sentences presuppose their *because*-clause. This roughly means that the mechanism to derive (50) from (49) is similar to that to derive (42) from (41) or (44) from (43): in all these cases, the notions of privative opposition and of the marked member of the opposition are essential.

I am not sure whether the mechanism used to derive rhetorical readings from some questions is the same as the mechanism to derive indirect speech acts in the above sense. The fact that the speaker needs to reconstruct the expression (or the expressions) the presupposition of which is given should probably be accounted for in psychological terms. Similarly, a psychological interpretation may also help to explain the cases I have discussed in chapter 4, namely that of the derivation of the illocutionary force of an order from the expression which presupposes the falsity of its base, or the case of the derivation of surprise or of amazement from the expression presupposing its base.

On the other hand, the derivation of the rhetorical reading seems to involve purely logical and semantic tools, such as the scope of negation, opacity, implication, declaration, or privative opposition.

I hope it is clear why I have spent so much time to present the various properties of privative oppositions: in my opinion, they lie at the basis of all essential phenomena the semantics of natural language meets with. For instance, in addition to the problems I have already discussed, think of the case of generic sentences. There are many indications suggesting that generic sentences are privatively opposed to their specific counterparts, and consequently, generic sentences may also be treated by means of privative oppositions.

An adequate treatment of privative oppositions encompasses, on the one hand, a formalization of the notion of disjunctive implication and, on the other hand, handling the opacity preserving negation and opaque operators in general in non-opaque contexts. Indeed, as we have seen, it is often necessary to calculate the negation of complex sentences in which binary sentential operators occur. For instance, we need to know what the normal negation is of (51), which I supposed to be equivalent to (52):

(51)   A knows whether P.

(52)   A knows that P or Bill knows that *not-P*.

Since (52) is an exclusive disjunction, its ordinary negation is roughly given in (53):

(53)   [A knows P and A knows *not-P*] or [A does not know P and A does not-know *not-P*].

But (53) seems to have two contradictory presuppositions, P and *not-P*, and consequently it cannot be the normal negation of (51).

Even if in (53) more has been done than is allowed by propositional calculus, this example shows that it is necessary to establish what the combination of opaque and non-opaque operators leads to and to investigate the degree of opacity of various complex operators, composed of non-opaque and opaque operators with different degrees of opacity. This is in particular obligatory for the combination of opaque sentences, because it is possible to conjoin indirect sentences of various types.

The solution of most of the above problems is subject to a semantic theory that underlies a theory of non-declarative sentences whose elements have been proposed here. What the semantics of non-declaratives will look like is far from obvious as it is far from obvious what kind of semantic theory natural language needs in general. What seems to be beyond doubt is that various implicative relations should be accounted for.

Much progress in the study of implicative relations, albeit of a reduced variety, has been accomplished within the so-called Montague semiotic program. Within this framework, research has been done also in the domain of non-declarative sentences: for instance, Belnap (1982) treats questions ans answers, Ik-Hwan (1982) attempts to provide an explicit syntax and semantics of imperative sentences, and Zaefferer (1983) tries to apply Montaque's semantics to the analysis of German exclamative sentences. Furthermore, Hausser (1980) tries to extend the principles of logical sementics to non-declarative sentence mood, and Groenendijk and Stokhof (1982) offer an analysis of some indirect non-declaratives with the help of an enriched intensional logic. Now, it is well-known that there is an important part of natural language which poses a problem for any semantic theory derived from logical semantics: belief-sentences, and more generally opaque sentences cannot be treated by the methods of Montague semantics (cf. Partee 1982). Since opaque sentences are fundamental for my analysis of non-declarative sentences and probably for declarative sentences as well, given the notion of presupposition I am making use of, any effort to adapt Montague's tools may seem hopeless.

Interestingly enough, the road does not seem entirely blocked since the intensional semantic relations I have described are always relations between syntactically related sentences. This means that, in general, it is not necessary to provide complete truth conditions for the implying sentence but truth conditions relative to the given implied sentence, which has arguments in common with the implying sentence that are important for opacity. In other words, according to my proposal, it is not necessary to 'enumerate' all potentially possible semantic consequences, but only those which are syntactically related to the implying sentence. If, in addition, we impose the condition that semantic consequences should be syntactically no more complex than the implying sentences, then the number of non-trivial semantic consequences will be finite. This leaves us with a huge field of investigation without having to face the basic objections the application of formal semantics to opaque sentences faces.

So let us come back to our language L and formulate some questions which we want our theory of non-declaratives to provide answers to. Suppose we have a suitable definition of the notion of presupposition in L. Then it would be interesting to find out the following:

(a)   Are there basic sentences which presuppose themselves?

(b)   Is a transformed sentence, which presupposes the basic sentence from which it was obtained, necessarily a non-basic sentence?

Let us now call the transformation which produces a non-basic sentence that cannot be embedded in an opaque operator an *intensional transformation*. Furthermore, let us call a non-basic sentence which presupposes a non-trivial Boolean combination of the basic sentence from which it was obtained a *non-declarative sentence*. Since there are three non-trivial Boolean combinations of a given basic sentence, there are three types of non-declarative sentences: *questions*, which disjunctively and maximally presuppose their base and its negation; *orders*, which maximally presuppose the negation of their base; and *exclamations*, which maximally presuppose their base. Given these definitions, the following questions are important:

(c)   Can every non-declarative sentence be obtained by means of an intensional (purely syntactic) transformation?

(d)   Are there only three intensional transformations?

(e)   Can the opaque operators taking questions, orders, and exclamations as complements be independently semantically characterized?

Suppose now, in addition, that we manage to define the notion of privative opposition and to specify conditions on which a normal negation ceases to be opacity preserving. Then the following questions arise:

(f)   Can some interrogative sentences declare the negation of the presupposition determined by the marked counterpart of the corresponding indirect question?

(g)   Can some sentences, considered as presuppositions, declare sentences which presuppose them?

All these questions just summarize the basic ideas of an abstract, non-pragmatic, and homogeneous theory of all types of non-declarative sentences. They also clearly indicate how many problems remain to be examined.

FOOTNOTES

1. Notice that this fact may be not sufficient to show that some natural language operators are opaque because they may have a so-called *transparent* reading, on which it is not necessary for the subject of the main verb to be aware of the property expressed by the description present in the sentence. But, of course, the opacity can still be shown by substituting not just NP's but the whole sentence in the scope of the operator.

2. This definition of analytic sentences is different from the one proposed in Zuber (1978a), where I considered as analytic those sentences which presuppose themselves. This difference is due to the larger field of investigation of this book in that we are also dealing with non-declarative sentences and with their inherent semantic relations.

3. I have in mind here a very simple measure of complexity, namely the length of the sequence forming a sentence. I am quite aware of the fact that this notion of complexity may appear far from sufficient.

4. The description in (6) ignores the important problem of specifying the time of existence (or of 'coming' into existence) of the action. To specify this, our metalanguage must include an expression like *to exist immediately after*, for example.

5. Of course they may sometimes have the so-called rhetorical reading. On this reading, which requires very special conditions, I consider them still as non-declarative sentences, but they 'indirectly' declare something. See the concluding section for more details.

6. Positive and negative imperatives do not necessarily express orders of the same kind. The kind of order may depend on the semantics of the verb and its aspects. Thus, in Slavic languages, negative orders to be immediately obeyed are not possible with perfective verbs. This impossibility can be explained by a joint analysis of imperatives such as the one proposed here and of the perfective aspect. For more details, see Zuber (1975).

7. Notice that the claim that performative operators are opaque entails that some performative sentences may be false. This result is in contradiction with some conceptions of performative sentences, according to which they are verifiable by their use or they are true just because they exist.

8. By 'first generation of erotetic logicians', I mean logicians like Aqvist, Belnap, Hamblin, Harrah, Kubinski, and Stahl. Their work, as well as some more recent research in erotetic logic, is reviewed in Harrah (n.d.).

9. 'Mami' is a Japanese given name.

10. Notice that we have to do here not just with the replacement of the false presupposition by a true one. In fact, the presupposition 'changes in time' whereas the actions are supposed to last in time. This means that, for basic orders, the metalanguage describing the

semantics of imperatives should use such expressions as *true immediately before some point, true immediately after some point*, etc.

11. One can find similar examples from other languages in Haiman (1978).

12. Notice that, in fact, I did not establish that the expected presupposition is a *maximal* one. Conditional sentences may have other presuppositions coming from the consequent clause, but these are related to the antecedent clause (cf. Zuber 1979 b).

13. That (98) is a normal negation of (96) is far from obvious. We cannot, however, dwell on this since we do not know exactly what kind of causation is involved in (96).

14. Notice that is most cases, I considered complementizers as a part of sentential operators. From the syntactic point of view, this decision is rather arbitrary.

15. In some situations, where the antecedent of the derived conditionals are obviously true, we can continue the derivation. Thus, in the situation where (a) is true, we obtain (c) from (b):

(a)   You can close the door.
(b)   Can you close the door?
(c)   Close the door!

But this further step is context dependent, since it depends on the judgment of the speaker with respect to a particular situation.

REFERENCES

Ajdukiewicz, K.
1926   "Analiza semantyczna zdania pytajnego". Ruch Filozoficzny 10.194-195.

Belnap, N.D., Jr.
1982   "Questions and answers in Montague grammar". In S. Peters and E. Saarinen (eds.), 165-198.

Bierwisch, M.
1980   "Semantic structures and illocutionary force". In J.R. Searle, F. Kiefer, and M. Bierwisch (eds.), 1-35.

Bolinger, D.
1978   "Yes-no questions are not alternative questions". In H. Hiz (ed.), 87-105.

Elliot, C.
1974   "Toward a grammar of exclamations". Foundations of Language 11.231-246.

Gazdar, G.
1976   "On performative sentences". Semantikos 1:3.37-62.

Grimshaw, J.
1979   "Complement selection and the lexicon". Linguistic Inquiry 10:2.279-326.

Groenendijk, J. and Stokhof, M.
1982   "Semantic analysis of wh-complements". Linguistics and Philosophy 5:2. 175-234.

Haiman, J.
1978   "Conditionals are topics". Language 54:3.564-589.

Hamblin, C.L.
1958   "Questions". Australian Journal of Philosophy 36.159-168.

Harrah, D.
n.d.   "The logic of questions". To appear in a volume devoted to philosophical logic.

Hausser, R.
1980   "Surface compositionality and the semantics of mood". In J. Searle, F. Kiefer, and M. Bierwisch (eds.), 71-95.

Hintikka, J.
1974   "Questions about questions". In M.K. Munitz and P.K. Unger (eds.), Semantics and philosophy. New York: New York University Press, 103-158.

1978   "Answers to questions". In H. Hiz (ed.), 279-300.

Hiz, H. (ed.)
1978   Questions. Dordrecht: D. Reidel.

Ik-Hwan, L.
    1982   "Syntax and semantics in imperative sentences". Paper presented at the International Congress of linguists, Tokyo, September 1982.

Jacobson, R.
    1957   Shifters, verbal categories and the Russian verb. Cambridge: Harvard University Press.

Karttunen, L.
    1973   "Presuppositions of compound sentences". Linguistc Inquiry 4:2.169-193.

Keenan, E.L.
    1973   "Presupposition in natural logic". The Monist 53:3.344-370.

Keenan, E.L. and R.D. Hull
    1973   "The logical presuppositions of questions and answers". In D. Franck and J. Petöfi (eds.), Präsuppositionen in Philosophie und Linguistik. Frankfurt: Athenaeum, 441-466.

Kubinski, T.
    1971   Wstep do logicznej teorii pytan. Warsaw: PWN.

Lang, R.
    1978   "Questions as epistemic requests". In H. Hiz (ed.), 301-318.

Mc Cawley, J.D.
    1981   Everything that linguists have always wanted to know about logic – but were ashamed to ask. Chicago: University of Chicago Press.

Partee, B.H.
    1982   "Belief-sentences and the limits of semantics". In S. Peters and E. Saarinen (eds.), 87-106.

Peters, S. and E. Saarinen (eds.)
    1982   Processes, beliefs, and questions. Dordrecht: D. Reidel.

Searle, J.R., F. Kiefer, and M. Bierwisch (eds.)
    1980   Speech act theory and pragmatics. Dordrecht: D. Reidel.

Stalnaker, R.
    1969   "A theory of conditionals". In N. Rescher (ed.), Studies in logical theory. Oxford: Blackwell, 98-112.

Wachowicz, K.
    1978   "Q-morpheme hypothesis". In H. Hiz (ed.), 151-163.

Wachtel, T.
    1979   "A question of imperatives". Papers and Studies in Contrastive Linguistics 10.5-31.

Wunderlich, D.
    1981   "Questions about questions". In W. Klein and W. Levelt (eds.), Crossing the boundaries in linguistics. Dordrecht: D. Reidel.

Zaefferer, D.
    1983   "The semantics of non-declaratives: Investigating German exclamatories. In

R. Bäuerle, Ch. Schwarze, and A. von Stechow (eds.), Meaning, use and interpretation. Berlin: de Gruyter, 466-490.

n.d.   "The semantics of sentence mood in typologically differing languages". To appear in the Proceedings of the XIIIth International Congress of Linguists.

Zuber, R.

1975   "Logic and grammar: An illustration from the Russian verbal aspect". Linguistische Berichte 39.22-27.

1976   "Knowing and analyticity". Logique at Analyse 75/76.219-222.

1977   "Decomposition of Factives". Studies in Language 1:3.407-421.

1978a   "Analyticity and genericness". Grazer Philosophische Studien 6.63-73.

1978b   "Review of 'Questions', H. Hiz (ed.)". Semantikos 2:2/3.95-100.

1979a   "Sign transparency and performatives". Semiotica 28.327-331.

1979b   "Towards a semantic description of logical connectives". Revue Roumaine de Linguistique 24:2.149-159.

1980a   "Privative opposition as a semantic relation". Journal of Pragmatics 4.413-424.

1980b   "Statut sémantique des actes indirects". Communications 32.240-249.

1980c   "Note on why factives cannot assert what their complement sentences express". Semantikos 4:2.79-80.

1981   "Mood markers and explicit performatives". Cahiers de Linguistique Française 3.35-47.

1982   "Some universal constraints on the semantic content of complex sentences". In R. Dirven and G. Radden (eds.), Issues in the theory of universal grammar. Tübingen: Gunter Narr Verlag, 145-157.

1983a   Non-declarative sentences. Amsterdam: John Benjamins

1983b   "Privative oppositions and intensional equivalence". Paper presented at the 7th International Congress for Logic, Methodology and Philosophy of Science, Salzburg, July 1983.

n.d.   "Generalizing presuppositions". Forthcoming.

In the PRAGMATICS & BEYOND series the following monographs have been published thus far:

I:1.   *Anca: M. Nemoianu*: The Boat's Gonna Leave: A Study of Children Learning a Second Language from Conversations with Other Children.
Amsterdam, 1980, vi, 116 pp. Paperbound.

I:2.   *Michael D. Fortescue*: A Discourse Production Model for 'Twenty Questions'.
Amsterdam, 1980, x, 137 pp. Paperbound.

I:3.   *Melvin Joseph Adler*: A Pragmatic Logic for Commands.
Amsterdam, 1980, viii, 131 pp. Paperbound.

I:4.   *Jef Verschueren*: On Speech Act Verbs.
Amsterdam, 1980, viii, 83 pp. Paperbound.

I:5.   *Geoffrey N. Leech*: Explorations in Semantics and Pragmatics.
Amsterdam, 1980, viii, 133 pp. Paperbound.

I:6.   *Herman Parret*: Contexts of Understanding.
Amsterdam, 1980, viii, 109 pp. Paperbound.

I:7.   *Benoît de Cornulier*: Meaning Detachment.
Amsterdam, 1980, vi, 124 pp. Paperbound.

I:8.   *Peter Eglin*: Talk and Taxonomy: A methodological comparison of ethnosemantics and ethnomethodology with reference to terms for Canadian doctors.
Amsterdam, 1980, x, 125 pp. Paperbound.

II:1.   *John Dinsmore*: The Inheritance of Presupposition.
Amsterdam, 1980, vi, 116 pp. Paperbound.

II:2.   *Charles Travis*: The True and the False: The Domain of the Pragmatic.
Amsterdam, 1980, vi, 116 pp. Paperbound.

II:3.   *Johan Van der Auwera*: What do we talk about when we talk? Speculative grammar and the semantics and pragmatics of focus.
Amsterdam, 1980, vi, 116 pp. Paperbound.

II:4.   *Joseph F. Kess & Ronald A. Hoppe*: Ambiguity in Psycholinguistics.
Amsterdam, 1980, vi, 116 pp. Paperbound.

II:5.   *Karl Sornig*: Lexical Innovation: A study of slang, colloquialisms and casual speech.
Amsterdam, 1980, vi, 116 pp. Paperbound.

II:6.   *Knud Lambrecht*: Topic, Antitpoic and Verb Agreement in Non-Standard French.
Amsterdam, 1980, vi, 116 pp. Paperbound.

II:7.   *Jan-Ola Östman*: 'You Know': A discourse-functional study.
Amsterdam, 1980, vi, 116 pp. Paperbound.

II:8.   *Claude Zilberberg*: Essai sur les modalités tensives.
Amsterdam, 1980, vi, 116 pp. Paperbound.

III:1. *Ivan Fonagy*: Situation et signification.
Amsterdam, 1980, vi, 116 pp. Paperbound.

III:2/3. *Jürgen Weissenborn and Wolfgang Klein (eds.)*: Here and There. Cross-linguistic Studies in Deixis and Demonstration.
Amsterdam, 1982. vi, 296 pp. Paperbound.

III:4. *Waltraud Brennenstuhl*: Control and Ability. Towards a Biocybernetics of Language.
Amsterdam, 1982. vi, 123 pp. Paperbound.